**SCHOLASTIC**

# GET READY FOR
# 3RD GRADE

Cover design by Josue Castilleja; Cover art by Bernard Adnet

ISBN 0-439-60627-6
Copyright © 2004 by Scholastic Inc. All rights reserved. Printed in the U.S.A.

3 4 5 6 7 8 9 10     40     09 08 07 06

New York • Toronto • London • Auckland • Sydney
Mexico City • New Delhi • Hong Kong • Buenos Aires

**Teaching** *Resources*

# Table of Contents

## Dear Parent:

Congratulations! You hold in your hands an exceptional educational tool that will give your child a head start into the coming school year.

Inside this book, you'll find one hundred practice pages that will help your child review and learn reading and writing skills, grammar, addition and subtraction, and so much more! *Get Ready for 3rd Grade* is divided into 10 weeks, with two practice pages for each day of the week, Monday to Friday. However, feel free to use the pages in any order that your child would like. Here are other features you'll find inside:

- A weekly **incentive chart** to motivate and reward your child for his or her efforts.

- A sheet of **colorful stickers** to add to the incentive chart. There are small stickers for completing the activities each day, as well as a large sticker to use as a weekly reward.

- Suggestions for fun, creative **learning activities** you can do with your child each week.

- A **recommended reading list** of age-appropriate books that you and your child can read throughout the summer.

- A **super-fun, full-color game board** that folds out from the back of the book. You'll also find a sheet of game cards and playing pieces.

- A **certificate of completion** to celebrate your child's accomplishments.

We hope you and your child will have a lot of fun as you work together to complete this workbook.

Enjoy!
**The editors**

# Terrific Tips for Using This Book

**1** Pick a good time for your child to work on the activities. You may want to do it around mid-morning after play, or early afternoon when your child is not too tired.

**2** Make sure your child has all the supplies he or she needs, such as pencils and crayons. Set aside a special place for your child to work.

**3** At the beginning of each week, discuss with your child how many minutes a day he or she would like to read. Write the goal at the top of the incentive chart for the week. (We recommend reading 15 to 20 minutes a day with your child who is entering 3rd grade.)

**4** Reward your child's efforts with the small stickers at the end of each day. As an added bonus, let your child affix a large sticker at the bottom of the incentive chart for completing the activities each week.

**5** Encourage your child to complete the worksheet, but don't force the issue. While you may want to ensure that your child succeeds, it's also important that your child maintain a positive and relaxed attitude toward school and learning.

**6** For more summertime fun, invite your child to play the colorful, skills-based game board at the back of the book. Your child can play the game with you or with friends and siblings.

**7** When your child has finished the workbook, present him or her with the certificate of completion at the back of the book. Feel free to frame or laminate the certificate and display it on the wall for everyone to see. Your child will be so proud!

# Helping Your Child Get Ready: Week 1

These are the skills your child will be working on this week.

## Math
- adding 1- and 2-digit numbers with regrouping
- subtracting 2-digit numbers without regrouping

## Reading
- classifying
- sequencing

## Writing
- sentence punctuation
- proofreading

## Vocabulary
- examining similarities
- sight words

## Grammar
- compound nouns

**Here are some activities you and your child might enjoy.**

**Sizzling Synonyms!** The first time your child says, "It's hot outside," challenge him or her to come up with as many words possible that mean the same thing as hot. You can try this with other weather words such as rainy or cloudy.

**Summer Goal** Suggest that your child come up with a plan to achieve a goal by the end of the summer. For example, he or she may wish to become an expert on a favorite animal or learn to count in another language. Help him or her map out a way to be successful. Periodically, check to see how your child is progressing.

**Order, Order!** Play a ranking game. Choose three related items and ask your child to put them in order. Ask him or her to explain the choice. For example, if you chose ice cube, snow ball, and frozen lake, your child might say small, medium, and large; or cold, colder, coldest.

**Sun Safety** Talk about sun safety with your child. Ask him or her to write a list of ways to stay safe in the sun. Post it in a prominent place!

**Your child might enjoy reading the following books.**

*Bringing the Rain to Kapiti Plain*
by Verna Aardema

*The New Kid on the Block*
by Jack Prelutsky

*Coming to America:*
*The Story of Immigration*
by Betsy Maestro

_____ **'s Incentive Chart: Week 1**

Name Here

This week, I plan to read _____ minutes each day.

CHART YOUR PROGRESS HERE.

| Week 1 | Day 1 | Day 2 | Day 3 | Day 4 | Day 5 |
|--------|-------|-------|-------|-------|-------|
| I read for... | minutes | minutes | minutes | minutes | minutes |
| Put a sticker to show you completed each day's work. | | | | | |

# Congratulations!

Wow! You did a great job this week!

#1

Place sticker here.

**Parent or Caregiver's Signature** _____

# Things We Use

People use different tools to do things. Read the list.

Draw a line from each player to the things for that sport.

1. **baseball player**

2. **football player**

3. **tennis player**

4. **cyclist**

5. **hockey player**

 **Talk with someone about how each thing is used.**

# Adding Words

A **compound noun** is made up of two smaller words put together.

**cup** + **cake** = **cupcake**

Can you figure out what these compound nouns are?
Read the clues. Then write the compound noun.

1. A **cloth** that covers a **table** is a _____

2. **Corn** that goes **pop** is _____

3. A **book** for a **cook** is a _____

4. An **apple** made into **sauce** is _____

5. A **cake** with **fruit** in it is a _____

6. **Meat** made into a **ball** is a _____

7. A **melon** with lots of **water** in it is a _____

8. A **berry** that is **blue** is a _____

Write a menu for a meal you would like. Use some compound nouns in your menu.

Scholastic Teaching Resources   Get Ready for 3rd Grade

# Kaleidoscope

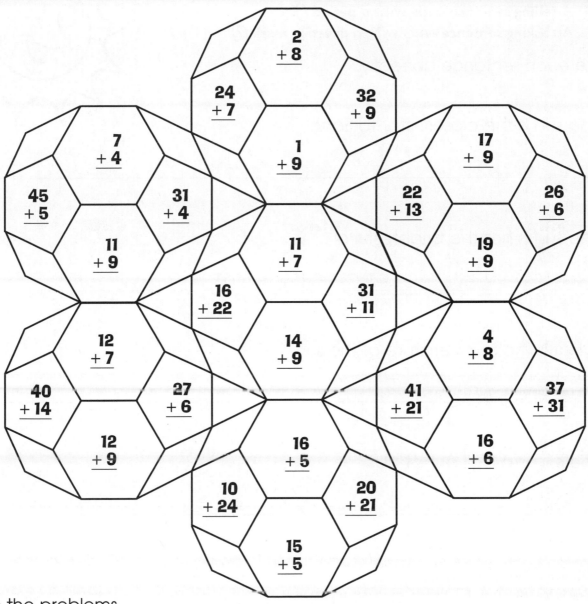

Solve the problems.

If the answer is between 1 and 30, color the shape red.

If the answer is between 31 and 99, color the shape gray.

Finish by coloring the other shapes with the colors of your choice.

Extra: Name two numbers that when added together equal 27.

# Sunny Sentences

 *Every sentence begins with a capital letter.
A telling sentence ends with a period (.).
An asking sentence ends with a question mark (?).*

Rewrite each sentence correctly.

1. the sun is the closest star to Earth

   _____

2. the sun is not the brightest star

   _____

3. what is the temperature of the sun

   _____

4. the sun is a ball of hot gas

   _____

5. how large is the sun

   _____

6. will the sun ever burn out

   _____

Scholastic Teaching Resources   *Get Ready for 3rd Grade*

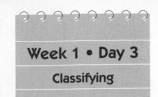

# Which One Doesn't Belong?

*Look for similarities when grouping items.*

Read each list. Cross out the word that doesn't belong. Then choose a word from the kite that belongs with each list and write it in the blank.

1. grouchy    mad       cheerful    fussy       _____

2. north       away      east        south       _____

3. goat        blue jay   robin       eagle       _____

4. juice       milk       tea         mud         _____

5. hand        toy        foot        head        _____

6. David       Bob        Ronald      Sarah       _____

7. spinach     cake       cookies     pie         _____

8. glue        bicycle    pencils     scissors    _____

9. penny       nickel     quarter     marble      _____

arm
dime
George
pudding
lemonade
parakeet
crayons
angry
west

Now read these categories. In each box, write the number from the above list that matches the category.

| Birds | Desserts | Bad Feelings |
|-------|----------|--------------|
| Boys' Names | Money | School Supplies |
| Directions | Body Parts | Drinks |

**Write a list of five things that go with this category: Things That Are Hot.**

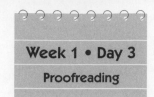

# A Happy Camper

➡️ *Complete:*
*Every sentence begins with a* _____.
*A statement ends with a* _____.
*A question ends with a* _____.

Uh oh! Dalton was in a hurry when he wrote this letter. Help him find 10 mistakes. Circle them.

Dear Mom and Dad,

camp is so cool? today we went swimming? do you know what the best part of camp is. i think fishing is my favorite thing to do. did you feed my hamster. I really miss you?

Love, Dalton

Now choose two questions and two statements from Dalton's letter. Rewrite each correctly.

1. _____

2. _____

3. _____

4. _____

 **On another piece of paper, write a letter to a friend or family member. Include two statements and two questions.**

12

Scholastic Teaching Resources  *Get Ready for 3rd Grade*

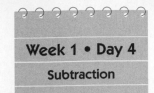
# Super Star

Solve the problems. If the answer is between 1 and 20, color the shape red. If the answer is between 21 and 40, color the shape white. If the answer is between 41 and 90, color the shape blue.

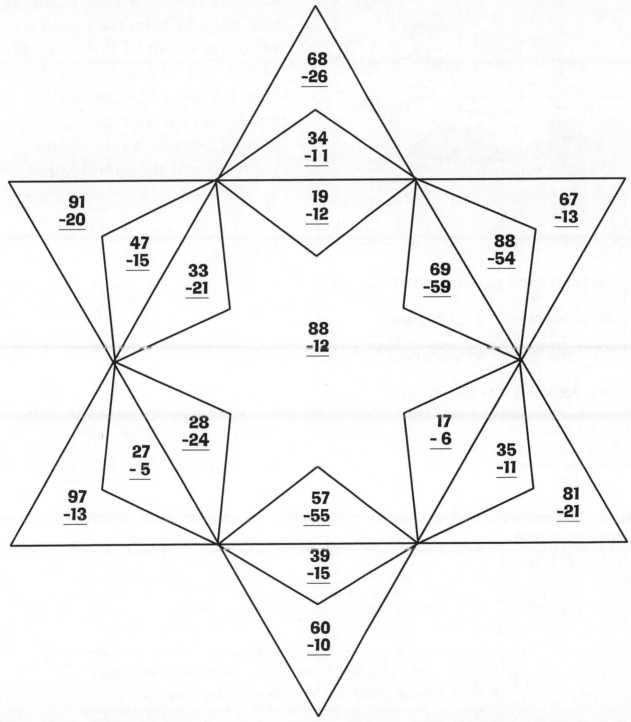

**Write five subtraction problems that have answers between 10 and 20.**

# Hello, Island!

About 30 years ago, some fishermen were on their boat near Iceland. Suddenly they saw smoke coming from the sea. Then the top of a volcano rose out of the water. Soon red-hot rock began to pour down its sides. It looked like the sea was on fire. At last the volcano cooled down. It became a new island. People named the island Surtsey.

Read how the island of Surtsey was made. Show the correct order of what happened. Write the numbers from 1–4 on the lines.

____ **Red-hot rock poured down its sides.**

____ **Smoke came out of the sea.**

____ **The new island was named Surtsey.**

____ **The volcano cooled down.**

Fill in the circles in order. Use the numbers and sentences above to help you. The first one is done for you.

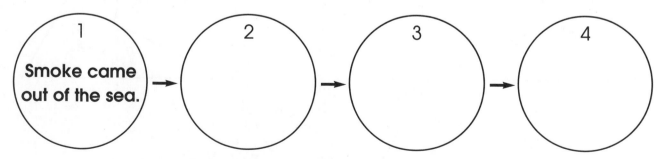

**1** Smoke came out of the sea. → **2** → **3** → **4**

 **Tell someone how Surtsey became an island. Draw pictures to show what happened.**

Scholastic Teaching Resources    *Get Ready for 3rd Grade*

# Turn on the Lights

Lighthouses warn ships that are near land. The first lighthouses were fires. People would build the fires on hilltops along the coast. Later people built towers. The light from their candles could be seen from far away. Then oil lamps were used. Today electricity runs a lighthouse's powerful lamps.

← lamp

← tower

Read how lighthouses changed.

Show the correct order of what happened. Write the numbers from 1–4 on the lines.

____ **Oil lamps lit lighthouses.**

____ **Lighthouses use electric light.**

____ **Fires were built on hillsides.**

____ **Candles were used.**

Fill in the circles in order. Use the numbers and sentences above to help you.

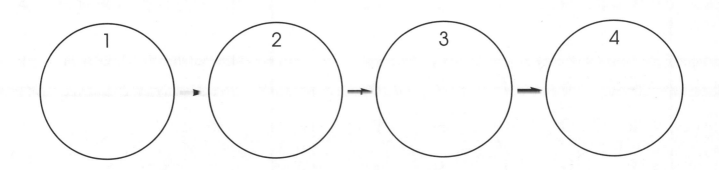

MORE! **Read *The Little Red Lighthouse* and the *Great Gray Bridge* by Hildegarde Swift.**

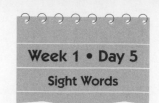

# Find the Word

Complete the sentences below with words from the Word Box. Then find the words in the puzzle. Words may go across, down, or diagonally. We did the first one for you.

1. I chose a pumpkin that had no bumps and was perfectly __round__ .

2. Sarah had a question about her homework, so she picked up the phone to _____ Tanisha.

3. After Juan ate the hot fudge sundae, his stomach felt very _____ .

4. When my mom went _____ on a trip, she sent me postcards.

5. Miko's cat likes to sit _____ her lap while Miko reads.

6. Sam had to _____ on his dog's leash to keep him away from the hornet's nest.

| A | R | H | L | U | I |
|---|---|---|---|---|---|
| D | W | L | U | P | P |
| I | A | A | D | O | U |
| C | E | F | Y | N | L |
| R | O | U | N | D | L |
| P | U | F | U | L | L |

**Word Box**

| away | ~~round~~ |
|------|-------|
| pull | full |
| call | upon |

Scholastic Teaching Resources   *Get Ready for 3rd Grade*

# Helping Your Child Get Ready: Week 2

These are the skills your child will be working on this week.

**Math**
- subtracting 2-digit numbers with regrouping
- adding 3-digit numbers with regrouping

**Reading**
- making inferences
- comprehension

**Writing**
- adjectives
- sentence punctuation

**Vocabulary**
- rhyming words
- part/whole analogies

**Grammar**
- subject/verb agreement
- present tense

**Handwriting**
- uppercase cursive letters

**Here are some activities you and your child might enjoy.**

**Scrambled Summer** Have your child write the words *summer vacation* on a sheet of paper and cut apart the letters. Encourage your child to use the letters to make new words. For variety, your child might also use the names of animals such as elephant, alligator, or hippopotamus.

**Terrific Time Lines** Help your child practice sequencing by creating time lines. For example, he or she can create a time line of the daily routine. Encourage him or her to write sentences to describe what happens first, next, and so on. Challenge your child to create a time line that includes the week's events, or one that shows at least one important event that occurred in each year of your child's life.

**Rhyme Relay** Pick a word, such as cat or dog, to begin a rhyme relay. Take turns with your child saying another word that rhymes with it.

**Newspaper Scavenger Hunt** You can use a newspaper for many different scavenger hunts. For example, ask your child to find a certain number of proper nouns, adjectives, quotation marks, or exclamation points. Or, you may wish to challenge your child to find different parts of a newspaper, such as headlines, political cartoons, or captions.

**Your child might enjoy reading the following books.**

*Black Cat*
by Christopher Meyers

*Dr. De Soto*
by William Steig

*Knots on a Counting Rope*
by John Archambault

_____ 's Incentive Chart: Week 2

Name Here

This week, I plan to read _____ minutes each day.

CHART YOUR PROGRESS HERE.

| Week 2 | Day 1 | Day 2 | Day 3 | Day 4 | Day 5 |
|---|---|---|---|---|---|
| I read for... | minutes | minutes | minutes | minutes | minutes |
| Put a sticker to show you completed each day's work. | | | | | |

Congratulations!

Wow! You did a great job this week!

#1

Place sticker here.

**Parent or Caregiver's Signature** _____

*a–z*

A B C D E F
G H I J K L M
N O P Q R S T
U V W X Y Z

Write.

# Figure It Out

Read each sentence. Then color the numbered space in the picture that matches the number of the correct answer.

**He rode his bike.**
**Who rode it?**
1. a boy
2. a girl

**Let's throw snowballs!**
**What time of year is it?**
3. summer
4. winter

**Run, John, run!**
**What sport is John in?**
5. swimming
6. track

**Please bait my hook.**
**What am I doing?**
7. fishing
8. playing baseball

**Breakfast is ready!**
**What time is it?**
9. night
10. morning

**I'm so thirsty.**
**What will I do?**
11. drink something
12. eat something

**Sorry! I broke it.**
**What could it be?**
13. a stuffed animal
14. a crystal vase

**He's a professor.**
**What is he?**
15. an adult
16. a baby

**It won't fit in the car.**
**What is it?**
17. a football
18. a swing set

**Look at the dark cloud.**
**Where should you look?**
19. down
20. up

**The lamb lost its mother.**
**Who is its mother?**
21. a sheep
22. a horse

**She wore a red hat.**
**Who wore it?**
23. a man
24. a woman

**I see a thousand stars.**
**What time is it?**
25. noon
26. night

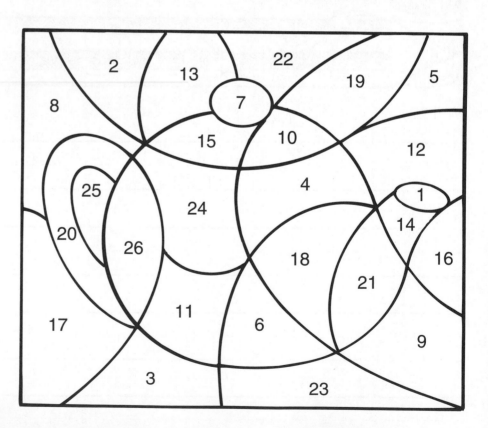

**Riddle: What begins with T, ends with T, and has T in it?**
**Find it in the puzzle.**

Scholastic Teaching Resources  *Get Ready for 3rd Grade*

# Up the Elephant's Trunk

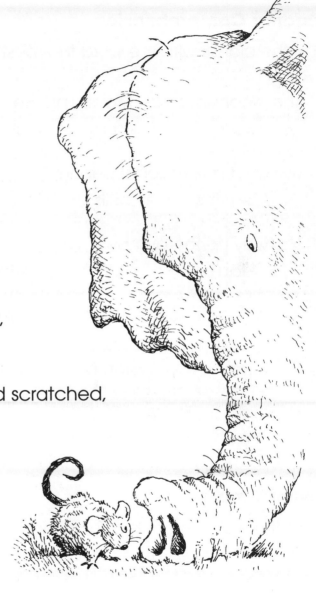

The elephant once said to me,
"Mouse, please climb in my nose
And go until I say to stop,
Then scratch there with your toes."

I climbed inside the long, deep trunk,
The air was damp and gray.
I walked across some peanut shells
And grass and bits of hay.

Then halfway up the bumpy trail
The elephant yelled, "Stop!"
"Scratch!" he said. "With all your might,
Just jump and kick and hop."

I scratched and itched and itched and scratched,
He finally yelled, "Enough!"
And then he blew me out his trunk
With lots of other stuff.

The elephant gave one big laugh
And said, "I thank you much."
And then he put his trunk on me
And gave me a warm touch.

☆ SPECIAL WORDS ☆

| nose | long | trunk | damp | bumpy | trail |

# Up the Elephant's Trunk

## Reading Comprehension

Fill in the blanks with the word that best completes the sentence.

1.  The elephant said, "Mouse, please _____ inside my nose."
    walk          jump          climb          get

2.  I walked across some peanut _____ .
    crumbs          shells          leaves          butter

3.  Halfway up the bumpy _____ , the elephant yelled, "Stop!"
    road          path          street          trail

4.  "Scratch!" he said. "With all your might, just jump and kick and
    _____ ."
    hop          stomp          step          fall

5.  He finally _____ , "Enough!"
    said          cried          yelled          shouted

## Rhyme Time

Circle the words in each column that rhyme with the word in bold. What other words rhyme with that word? Write them in the spaces below.

| nose | long | trunk | damp | bumpy | trail |
|------|------|-------|------|-------|-------|
| not  | song | dunk  | camp | lumpy | pail  |
| goes | lone | sunk  | ramp | humpy | sail  |
| bows | wrong| truck | dump | puppy | tail  |
| ____ | ____ | ____  | ____ | ____  | ____  |
| ____ | ____ | ____  | ____ | ____  | ____  |

Scholastic Teaching Resources   *Get Ready for 3rd Grade*

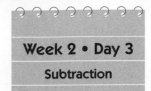
# Grandma's Quilt

Solve the problems. If the answer is between 1 and 50, color the shape red. If the answer is between 51 and 100, color the shape blue. Finish the design by coloring the other shapes with the colors of your choice.

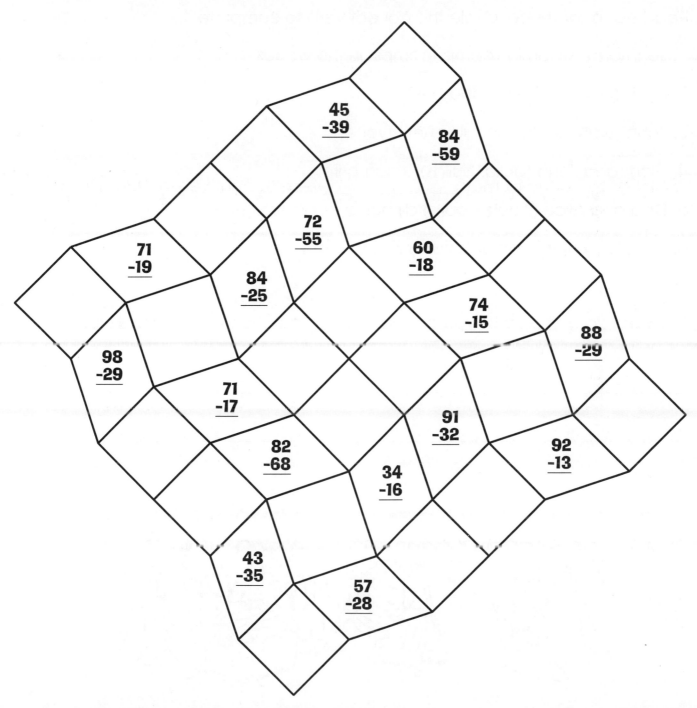

45
-39

84
-59

72
-55

71
-19

60
-18

84
-25

74
-15

88
-29

98
-29

71
-17

91
-32

92
-13

82
-68

34
-16

43
-35

57
-28

**Amelia bought 30 tickets for rides at the carnival. She used 15 tickets in the first hour. How many tickets did she have left?**

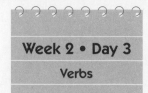

# How to Agree

If the naming part of a sentence is a noun or pronoun that names one, the verb ends in **-s**, except for the pronouns **I** and **you**. If the naming part is a noun or pronoun that names more than one, the verb does not end in **-s**.

Read each sentence. Circle the correct verb to complete it.

1. John and his family (camp, camps) in the woods.

2. Alice (like, likes) hiking the best.

3. John (walk, walks) ahead of everyone.

4. Mom and John (build, builds) a campfire.

5. Dad and Alice (cook, cooks) dinner over the fire.

6. Alice and Mom (crawl, crawls) into the tent.

Choose two of the verbs you circled. Write a sentence using each verb.

_____

_____

Scholastic Teaching Resources   *Get Ready for 3rd Grade*

# Draw a Picture

**Verbs** tell when action takes place. Present-tense verbs tell about action that is happening now. A verb showing the action of one person ends in **-s**. A verb telling the action of more than one person does not end in **-s**.

The boy sings.                                         The boys sing.

In the sentences below, underline each action verb. Then draw a picture that shows the action. Be sure to show if it is one person or animal doing the action or more than one person or animal doing the action.

| | |
|---|---|
| 1. **Four birds sit on the fence.** | 2. **That dog digs.** |
| 3. **A man sells hotdogs.** | 4. **The girls run.** |

Choose one of the pictures you drew. Write a short story about it.

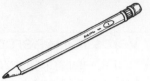

# Pick a Part

Circle the correct word to complete each sentence.

1. A leg is a part of a table, and a seat is a part of a _____.
   A. rug               B. chair               C. bed

2. A string is a part of a harp, and a button is a part of a _____.
   A. shirt             B. snap                C. circle

3. A screen is a part of a TV, and a hand is a part of a _____.
   A. broom             B. clock               C. knob

4. A yolk is a part of an egg, and a pit is a part of a _____.
   A. peach             B. hen                 C. word

5. A heel is a part of a foot, and an eye is a part of a _____.
   A. toe               B. nose                C. face

6. A stove is a part of a kitchen, and a couch is a part of a _____.
   A. den               B. sink                C. floor

7. A wing is a part of a bird, and a sleeve is a part of a _____.
   A. nest              B. sweater             C. pocket

8. A drawer is a part of a desk, and a pedal is a part of a _____.
   A. ladder            B. step                C. bike

 **Name two things that each of these can be a part of: ear, eye, arm, leg, and neck.**

Scholastic Teaching Resources   *Get Ready for 3rd Grade*

# Tricky Twins

Sandy and Mandy are having a twin party. There are six sets of twins, but only one set of identical twins. To find the identical twins, solve the addition problems under each person. The identical twins have the same answer.

207
+ 544

126
+ 89

328
+ 348

257
+ 458

547
+ 129

624
+ 127

108
+ 107

229
+ 418

258
+ 268

379
+ 336

417
+ 109

153
+ 494

# Seashore Sentences

Complete:

A _____ ends with a period.
A _____ ends with a question mark.
An _____ ends with an exclamation point.

Write a statement (S), a question (Q), and an exclamation (E) about each picture.

S _____

_____

Q _____

_____

E _____

_____

S _____

_____

Q _____

_____

E _____

_____

 **On another piece of paper, write a statement, a question, and an exclamation about a cartoon in the newspaper.**

# Helping Your Child Get Ready: Week 3

These are the skills your child will be working on this week.

**Math**
- simple equations
- adding 3-digit numbers with regrouping

**Reading**
- comprehension
- reading for details

**Writing**
- writing to a prompt

**Vocabulary**
- synonyms
- sight words

**Grammar**
- adjectives
- quotation marks

**Handwriting**
- lowercase cursive letters

### Here are some activities you and your child might enjoy.

**Amusing Attributes** Riddles such as the following are great ways to exercise your child's thinking skills. Read each riddle and ask your child to figure out the common link.

Abby likes books. . . but not reading. She likes swimming. . . but not splashing. Abby likes napping. . . but not dozing. She also enjoys spaghetti. . . but not pasta. (Abby likes things that have double letters.)

Alex likes apples. . . but not fruit. He likes airplanes. . . but not jets. Alex likes August. . . but not summer. He also enjoys astronomy. . . but not stars. (Alex likes things that start with "A".)

**What's Your Estimate?** Ask your child to estimate how many times in 60 seconds he or she can . . .
**a)** say his or her full name    **b)** write the days of the week

Then have him or her try each activity and compare the results with the estimate.

**Imagine That!** Invite your child to close his or her eyes. Ask: *What sounds do you hear?* Can your child name ten?

**Amazing Animals** If your child could be any kind of animal, which one would he or she choose and why? Using lots of detail, have your child describe or draw ten reasons.

### Your child might enjoy reading the following books.

*Angel Child, Dragon Child*
by Michele Maria Surat

*Stringbean's Trip to the Shining Sea*
by Vera B. Williams

*The True Story of the Three Little Pigs*
by Jon Scieszka

_____**'s Incentive Chart: Week 3**

Name Here

This week, I plan to read _____ minutes each day.

CHART YOUR PROGRESS HERE.

| Week 3 | Day 1 | Day 2 | Day 3 | Day 4 | Day 5 |
|--------|-------|-------|-------|-------|-------|
|  I read for... | minutes | minutes | minutes | minutes | minutes |
| Put a sticker to show you completed each day's work. | ○ ○ | ○ ○ | ○ ○ | ○ ○ | ○ ○ |

# Congratulations!

Wow! You did a great job this week!

Place sticker here.

**Parent or Caregiver's Signature** _____

*a–z*

*a b c d e f g*

*h i j k l m*

*n o p q r s t*

*u v w x y z*

Write.

_____

_____

_____

_____

_____

_____

_____

_____

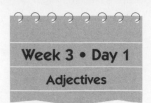

# Describe a Noun

An **adjective** describes a person, place, or thing. Color, size, and number words are adjectives.

Read each sentence. Find the adjective and the noun it describes. Circle the noun. Write the adjective on the line.

1. Peggy and Rosa went to the big zoo. _____

2. They looked up at the tall giraffe. _____

3. The giraffe looked down at the two girls. _____

4. The giraffe had brown spots. _____

Write adjectives from the sentences in the chart.

| Color Word | Size Words | Number Word |
|---|---|---|
| _____ | _____ | _____ |
| | _____ | |

Scholastic Teaching Resources   *Get Ready for 3rd Grade*

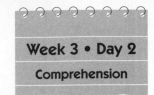
# Panda Pair

In 1972, Americans fell in love with two giant pandas named Hsing-Hsing and Ling-Ling. The pandas came to the United States from China. The National Zoo in Washington, D.C., became the pandas' new home. On their first day there, 20,000 people visited the two pandas. The crowds kept coming year after year.

Hsing-Hsing and Ling-Ling were just cubs when they got to the United States. As the years passed, many hoped the pair would have cubs of their own. Ling-Ling gave birth several times. But none of the babies lived more than a few days. Each time a cub died, people around the world felt sad.

Both pandas lived to an old age. Ling-Ling was 23 when she died in 1992. Hsing-Hsing died in 1999 at the age of 28. But the pandas were not forgotten. At the National Zoo, the glass walls of their home were covered with letters from children. The letters expressed the children's love for the pandas and told how much they were missed.

1. **The author wrote this passage mostly to:**
   A. tell about Hsing-Hsing and Ling-Ling.
   B. explain where giant pandas come from.
   C. describe a giant panda's cubs.
   D. convince people to visit the National Zoo.

2. **According to the author, how did people feel about the pandas?**

   _____

3. **If you visited the National Zoo in 2000, what would you have seen at the pandas' home?**

   _____

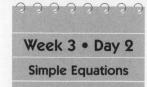

# Number Words

Write each sentence using numbers and symbols.

| | |
|---|---|
| 1. Four plus five is nine. | |
| 2. Eleven minus six is five. | |
| 3. Nine plus seven is sixteen. | |
| 4. Four plus eight is twelve. | |
| 5. Three minus two is one. | |
| 6. Seven plus seven is fourteen. | |
| 7. Fifteen minus ten is five. | |
| 8. Two plus eight is ten. | |
| 9. Five minus two is three. | |

# Who Is Speaking?

**Quotation marks** show the exact words someone says. They go before the speaker's first word. They also go after the speaker's last word and the end punctuation mark.

Read each sentence. Underline the exact words the speaker says. Put the words in quotation marks. The first one is done for you.

1. Max said, "Let's go on a picnic."

2. Cori replied, That's a great idea.

3. Andy asked, What should we bring?

4. Max said with a laugh, We should bring food.

5. Cori added, Yes, let's bring lots and lots of food.

6. Andy giggled and said, You're no help at all!

Finish the sentences below by writing what Max, Cori, and Andy might say next. Use quotation marks.

7. Max said, _____.

8. Cori asked, _____.

9. Andy answered, _____.

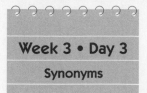

# Same As

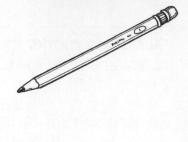

Circle the correct word to complete each sentence.

1. A stick is like a stake, and a cap is like a _____.
   A. sock          B. hat          C. twig

2. A runner is like a racer, and a smile is like a _____.
   A. frown          B. face          C. grin

3. A crowd is like a mob, and a song is like a _____.
   A. group          B. tune          C. flute

4. A dinner is like a supper, and a pot is like a _____.
   A. pan          B. cook          C. meal

5. Fur is like fuzz, and wet is like _____.
   A. messy          B. dry          C. damp

6. Sad is like gloomy, and happy is like _____.
   A. glad          B. mad          C. nice

7. Misty is like foggy, and fast is like _____.
   A. runner          B. quick          C. slow

8. Look is like see, and sleep is like _____.
   A. nap          B. wake          C. find

 **Discuss with someone why you did not choose the other words.**

Scholastic Teaching Resources    *Get Ready for 3rd Grade*

# Sandwich Shop

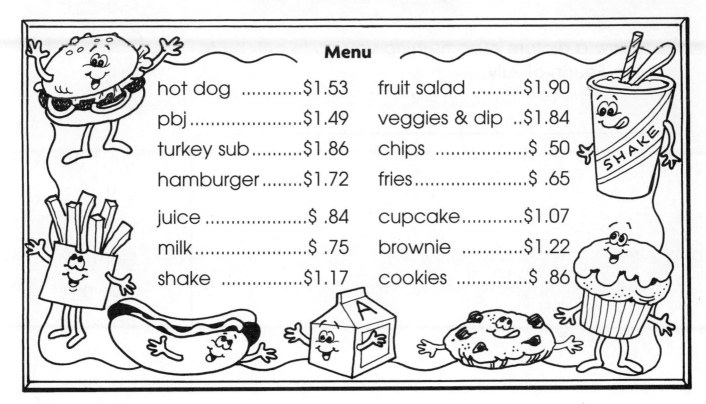

**Menu**

| | |
|---|---|
| hot dog ...........$1.53 | fruit salad .........$1.90 |
| pbj.....................$1.49 | veggies & dip ..$1.84 |
| turkey sub.........$1.86 | chips .................$ .50 |
| hamburger.......$1.72 | fries.....................$ .65 |
| juice .................$ .84 | cupcake...........$1.07 |
| milk....................$ .75 | brownie ...........$1.22 |
| shake .............$1.17 | cookies .............$ .86 |

Add.

**A.**

pbj
chips
milk
brownie        + 
_____

**B.**

hamburger
fries
shake        + 
_____

**C.**

turkey sub
veggies & dip
juice
cupcake        + 
_____

**D.**

hot dog
fruit salad
brownie
juice        + 
_____

**E.**

turkey sub
chips
shake        + 
_____

**F.**

pbj
cookies
milk        + 
_____

# Celebrating Our Country

 Draw a picture of something you do to celebrate the Fourth of July.

| Word Bank |
| --- |
| eat |
| play |
| swim |
| fireworks |
| cookout |
| picnic |
| beach |
| park |
| country |
| history |
| family |
| free |
| proud |
| happy |

On the Fourth of July, I _____

_____

I celebrate this holiday with _____

_____

On the Fourth of July, I also like to _____

_____

We celebrate this holiday because _____

_____

Scholastic Teaching Resources  *Get Ready for 3rd Grade*

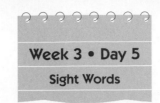

# Sort It Out!

Put each word from the Word Box in the circle where it belongs.
We did the first one for you.

**Word Box**

| | | |
|---|---|---|
| ~~found~~ | find | behind |
| away | upon | pull |
| call | put | above |
| below | around | |

**Action Words**

found
_____

_____

_____

_____

**Direction Words**

_____

_____

_____

_____

_____

_____

**Now try this!**

Write a sentence using as many words from the Word Box as you can.

_____

_____

How many words from the Word Box did you use? _____

# Fancy Fireworks

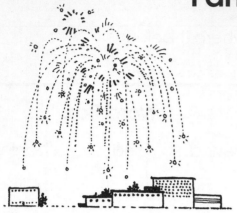

Kaboom! It's the Fourth of July. Fireworks light up the night. Have you ever seen a willow firework? It has long trails of color that float to the ground. The pinwheel and comet are two other popular fireworks. One of the loudest fireworks is called the salute. After a bright flash, you hear a loud BOOM!

Read the paragraph. Then answer the questions.

1. Which firework has long trails of color? _____

2. Which firework makes a loud BOOM? _____

3. What is a popular firework? _____

Add three more details to the web.

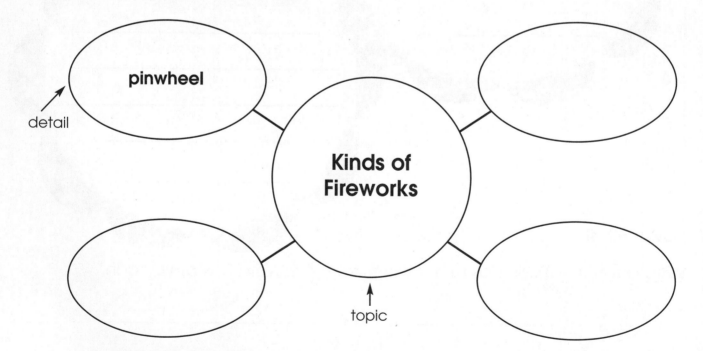

detail → **pinwheel**

**Kinds of Fireworks**

topic ↑

 **What do you think a pinwheel firework looks like? Draw a picture to show your ideas.**

Scholastic Teaching Resources    *Get Ready for 3rd Grade*

# Helping Your Child Get Ready: Week 4

These are the skills your child will be working on this week.

**Math**
- measurement
- multiplication

**Reading**
- reading for details
- comprehension

**Writing**
- expanding sentences
- adjectives

**Vocabulary**
- sight words

**Grammar**
- subject/verb agreement
- past tense

**Here are some activities you and your child might enjoy.**

**Compound Interest** Point out examples of compound words to your child. Then have him or her keep track of the compound words heard during an hour. Try it another time and challenge your child to improve on his or her last "score."

**Start Collecting** Having a collection is a great way for a child to develop higher-level thinking skills like sorting and analyzing. Encourage your child to start one. Leaves, rocks, stamps, or shells are all easy and fun things to collect. Your child can also practice comparing and contrasting by discussing how the items in his or her collection are similar and different from one another.

**The Case of the Mysterious Sock** Invite your child to find a secret object to put in a sock. Try to guess what it is by feeling the object through the sock. Trade places. Play again.

**Pet Autobiography** Suggest that your child write the story of your pet's (or an imaginary pet's) life. The story should be an autobiography—from the pet's point of view!

**Your child might enjoy reading the following books.**

*Dinner at Aunt Connie's House*
by Faith Ringgold

*The Family Under the Bridge*
by Natalie Savage Carlson

*Ramona Quimby, Age 8*
by Beverly Cleary

_____ 's Incentive Chart: Week 4

Name Here

This week, I plan to read _____ minutes each day.

CHART YOUR PROGRESS HERE.

| Week 4 | Day 1 | Day 2 | Day 3 | Day 4 | Day 5 |
|---|---|---|---|---|---|
| **I read for...** | minutes | minutes | minutes | minutes | minutes |
| Put a sticker to show you completed each day's work. | | | | | |

# Congratulations!

Wow! You did a great job this week!

#1

Place sticker here.

**Parent or Caregiver's Signature** _____

# What's for Lunch?

Have you ever had a string bean sandwich? Most students wouldn't want that for lunch! What is the favorite sandwich in America's school lunches? If you said peanut butter and jelly, you'd be right. Other popular sandwiches are ham and bologna. Cheese is the fourth favorite sandwich. Many students also like turkey sandwiches.

What is the topic of the paragraph?
Write it in the center circle.
Find five details that tell about the topic.
Write them in the web.

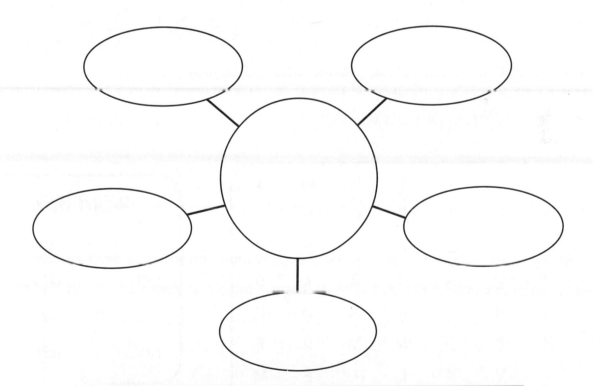

 **What kinds of sandwiches does your family like the best? Take a survey of your family.**

# Find the Word

Complete the sentences below with words from the Word Box. Then find the words in the puzzle. Words may go across, down, or diagonally. We did the first one for you.

1. Have you __thought__ about what you'd like for your birthday?

2. Hannah likes to _____ home from school.

3. Last Friday, I _____ a new notebook.

4. Today I will _____ the notebook to school with me.

5. Ruthie and Carlos like to _____ pictures of animals.

6. May I _____ your hand if I get scared during the movie?

7. Sometimes we _____ too loudly in the library.

8. Tanya used colored pencils when she _____ that picture.

| B | T | B | R | I | N | G | T |
|---|---|---|---|---|---|---|---|
| D | H | E | W | E | Q | H | S |
| R | O | J | O | Z | G | X | K |
| A | U | O | Q | U | R | L | B |
| W | G | H | O | E | A | D | P |
| D | H | B | O | W | M | R | F |
| P | T | V | K | L | L | E | M |
| T | A | L | K | S | D | W | F |

### Word Box

bought     drew

bring      draw

~~thought~~   walk

hold       talk

Scholastic Teaching Resources  Get Ready for 3rd Grade

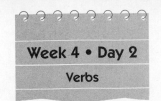
# What Happened?

If the naming part of a sentence is a noun or pronoun that names one, the verb ends in **-s**, except for the pronouns **I** and **you**. If the naming part is a noun or pronoun that names more than one, the verb does not end in **-s**.

Choose the correct action word from the box to complete each sentence. Write it on the line.

| play | run | dive | climb | throw |
|------|-----|------|-------|-------|
| plays | runs | dives | climbs | throws |

1. Mia _____ ball with her friends.

2. The children like to _____ together.

3. Juan _____ faster than I do.

4. We _____ on a track team.

5. Tom and Kara _____ into the pool.

6. Mary _____ without her goggles.

7. They _____ very tall trees.

8. Liz _____ steep mountains.

9. Juan and Mia _____ balls.

10. I _____ the ball to Juan.

She hops.

They hop.

# Football Frenzy

 *A sentence is more interesting when it gives exact information.*

Replace each 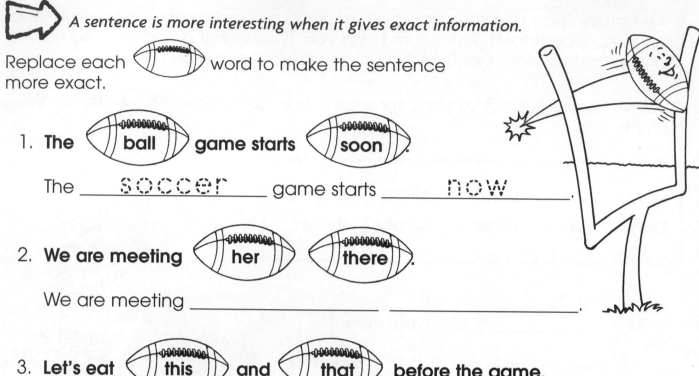 word to make the sentence more exact.

1. **The** ball **game starts** soon .

   The _____soccer_____ game starts _____now_____.

2. **We are meeting** her there .

   We are meeting _____ _____.

3. **Let's eat** this **and** that **before the game.**

   Let's eat _____ and _____ before

   the game.

4. **I hope** they **score** some **points.**

   I hope _____ score _____ points.

5. They **were also** there .

   _____ were also _____.

6. He **played a** good **game!**

   _____ played a _____ game!

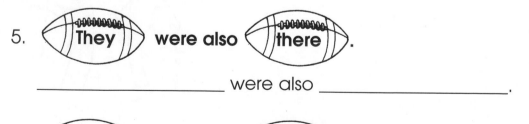

46

# Weight Watcher

Weight can be measured in ounces (oz.) and pounds (lb.). 16 oz. = 1 lb.
Which unit of measure would you use to weigh the items below? Underline
the more sensible measure.

1. An apple

    **ounces   pounds**

2. A pair of sneakers

    **ounces   pounds**

3. A bar of soap

    **ounces   pounds**

4. A bicycle

    **ounces   pounds**

5. A watermelon

    **ounces   pounds**

6. A baseball player

    **ounces   pounds**

7. A balloon

    **ounces   pounds**

8. A jam sandwich

    **ounces   pounds**

9. A baseball bat

    **ounces   pounds**

10. A pair of socks

    **ounces   pounds**

11. A slice of pizza

    **ounces   pounds**

12. A full backpack

    **ounces   pounds**

13. A large dog

    **ounces   pounds**

14. A loaf of bread

    **ounces   pounds**

15. A paintbrush

    **ounces   pounds**

# Lost and Found

Read the story. Then fill in the bubble next to the best answer to each question below.

One day Alisha's little brother found **three** dollars. "Look!" he said. "Now I can buy a pony!"

"I think a pony will cost too **much**," Alisha said. "**Shall** I help you **find** something to spend it on?"

"Okay," he said. He **put** the money in his pocket.

"Ice cream might be a good thing to spend it on," said Alisha. "What **kind** do you want?"

"I **only** like one kind. Chocolate," said her brother.

"I think chocolate is the best kind, **too**," said Alisha.

1. When Alisha says a pony will cost too **much**, she means
   - ○ a. Three dollars is more than enough money to buy a pony.
   - ○ b. A pony costs a lot more than three dollars.
   - ○ c. If her brother had found three dollars, he could buy a pony.

2. When Alisha says, "I think chocolate is the best kind, **too**," the word **too** means
   - ○ a. also.
   - ○ b. two.
   - ○ c. not at all.

3. The opposite of **found** is
   - ○ a. kept.
   - ○ b. forgot.
   - ○ c. lost.

4. Which word means the same as **kind** in this story?
   - ○ a. nice
   - ○ b. child
   - ○ c. type

5. In the dictionary, the word **only** appears
   - ○ a. between the words **lonely** and **quiet**.
   - ○ b. after the word **totally**.
   - ○ c. before the word **night**.

Scholastic Teaching Resources   *Get Ready for 3rd Grade*

# Letter From Vera

April 11

Dear Morey,

I just got your letter with the picture of you riding your bike. From the smile on your face, I can tell how much fun you're having. I still remember when you could hardly ride a tricycle. You've come a long way!

Now here's some advice. I'm sure you're a good rider. But you will fall off that bike now and then. So please get yourself a helmet. Wear it every time you ride. A helmet will help protect you from a head injury. Wearing a helmet when you ride a bike is as important as wearing your seat belt when you ride in a car!

No, I'm not trying to be a bossy know-it-all. I just don't want a bad fall to wipe that smile off your face. When you come to visit this summer, bring your bike and your helmet. We'll take some great rides together!

Your cousin,
Vera

1. **From this letter, what can you tell about the picture of Morey that he sent to Vera?**

   A. He is riding a tricycle.          C. He is in his driveway.

   B. He is not wearing a helmet.    D. He is looking scared.

2. **Vera's advice shows that she:**

   F. cares a lot about safety.      H. doesn't like riding bikes.

   G. is often bossy and mean.       J. is learning to drive a car.

3. **What will Morey do with Vera during the summer?**

   _____

   _____

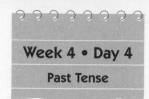

# A Verb Puzzle

**Verbs** tell when action takes place. Past-tense verbs tell about action that happened in the past. Most past-tense verbs end in **-ed**.

Write the past tense of each word in the box. Then use the past tense words to complete the puzzle below.

| | | |
|---|---|---|
| call _____ | mix _____ | play _____ |
| yell _____ | kick _____ | help _____ |
| bark _____ | climb _____ | walk _____ |

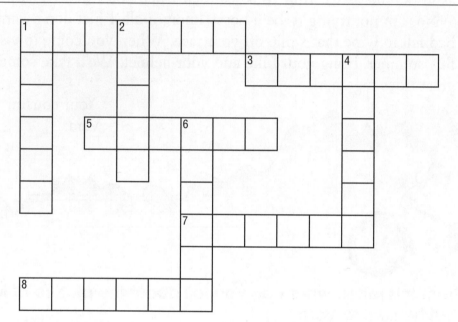

## Across

1. Mike _____ over the wall.
3. The dog _____.
5. Our teacher _____ us with the math problems.
7. We _____ at the team to win.
8. The boys _____ home from school.

## Down

1. Sam _____ his dad on the phone.
2. Grandma _____ the cake batter.
4. The player _____ the ball.
6. Marie _____ a game with Zack.

Write a sentence using each of the verbs from the puzzle.

# How Many Legs?

Fill in the blanks.

**1.** How many legs on

1 turkey _____     3 turkeys _____

2 turkeys _____     4 turkeys _____

**2.** How many legs on

1 cat _____     3 cats _____

2 cats _____     4 cats _____

**3.** How many legs on

1 ladybug _____     3 ladybugs _____

2 ladybugs _____     4 ladybugs _____

**4.** How many legs on

1 spider _____     3 spiders _____

2 spiders _____     4 spiders _____

**5.** How many legs on

1 squid _____     6 squid _____

2 squid _____     7 squid _____

3 squid _____     8 squid _____

4 squid _____     9 squid _____

5 squid _____     10 squid _____

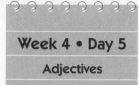
# Mystery Bags

 **Adjectives** *are words that help you imagine how something looks, feels, smells, sounds, or tastes.*

Make a list of words that describe the object in each bag below.

 **Use a paper sack to make a real mystery bag. Place an object in the bag and give describing clues to someone. Can he or she guess the mystery object?**

Scholastic Teaching Resources   *Get Ready for 3rd Grade*

# Helping Your Child Get Ready: Week 5

These are the skills your child will be working on this week.

**Math**
- multiplication
- number words

**Reading**
- compare/contrast

**Writing**
- combining sentences

**Vocabulary**
- homophones
- proofreading/spelling

**Grammar**
- verbs
- contractions

**Handwriting**
- cursive numbers 0–9

The New Bike
By Cindy Read
illustrations by Ana Rest

**Here are some activities you and your child might enjoy.**

**Carrot-Turnip-Pea** Develop your child's listening skills by creating a word chain. In this game, someone says a word, and the next person must say a word that begins with the last letter of the previous player's word. To make this more challenging, try choosing a category such as names or foods.

**Now You See It, Now You Don't** Show your child an interesting picture and ask him or her to look at it for a minute. Then turn the picture over and ask your child to list the objects that he or she can remember on a sheet of paper. If you wish, allow your child to look at the picture for another minute and then add more items to the list. For a twist, use a picture with less detail, but ask your child to list the words in alphabetical order.

**Secret Messages** Suggest that your child come up with a code to write secret messages. Have him or her trade messages with you or another family member.

**Can You Judge a Book by Its Cover?** Give your child a chance to create a new cover for a favorite book. Remind him or her to include the title, as well as the names of the author and any illustrator. Encourage your child to include an image or images that they think would inspire someone to read the book.

**Your child might enjoy reading the following books.**

*The Summer My Father Was Ten*
by Pat Brisson

*This Land Is Your Land*
by Woody Guthrie

*Falling Up*
by Shel Silverstein

_____ 's Incentive Chart: Week 5

Name Here

This week, I plan to read _____ minutes each day.

CHART YOUR PROGRESS HERE.

| Week 5 | Day 1 | Day 2 | Day 3 | Day 4 | Day 5 |
|---|---|---|---|---|---|
| I read for... | minutes | minutes | minutes | minutes | minutes |
| Put a sticker to show you completed each day's work. | | | | | |

# Congratulations!

Wow! You did a great job this week!

#1

Place sticker here.

**Parent or Caregiver's Signature** _____

# Foreign Flags

Every country has its own flag. Japan has a white flag with a red circle on it. The red circle stands for the sun. Japan's name means the "land of the rising sun." Canada also has a red and white flag. But its flag has a white background with two wide red stripes. In the center of the flag is a red maple leaf. The maple tree is a symbol of Canada.

Read the paragraph. Then answer the questions.

1. What colors are both flags? _____

2. What does Japan's flag have in the center? _____

3. What does Canada's flag have in the center? _____

4. How are the backgrounds of the two flags different? _____

Write your answers in the correct parts of the circles.

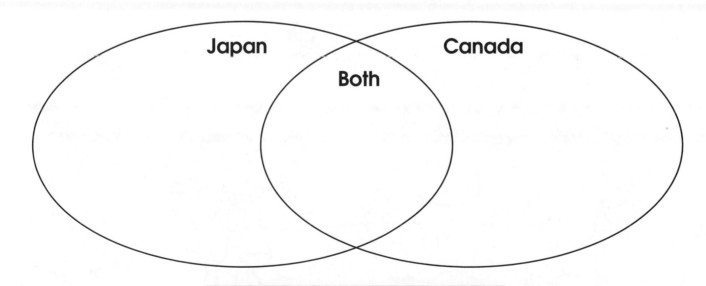

Japan    Both    Canada

 Find Japan and Canada on a world map.

# Verb *to be*

**Am**, **is**, **are**, **was**, and **were** are forms of the verb **to be**. These verbs show being instead of action.

Read each sentence. Underline the verb. Write **past** if the sentence tells about the past. Write **now** if the sentence tells about the present.

1. The story is perfect. _____

2. The producers are happy. _____

3. The actors were funny. _____

4. The movie studio is interested in the story. _____

5. I am excited about the movie. _____

6. I was sad at the end. _____

56

# Numbers 0-9

Trace and write.

0 0

1 1

2 2

3 3

4 4

5 5

6 6

7 7

8 8

9 9

# Field Trip Cars

1.

Josie's class is going to the teddy bear factory.
Three children will ride in each car.
Draw a circle around the children who will ride in each car.

How many cars do they need? _____

2.

Pete's class is going to see the elephant seals.
Five children will ride in each van.
Draw a circle around the children who will ride in each van.

How many vans do they need? _____

3.

Rosa's class is going to the Space Museum.
Eight children will ride in each small bus.
Draw a circle around the children who will ride in each bus.

How many small buses do they need? _____

Scholastic Teaching Resources    Get Ready for 3rd Grade

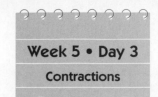
# Contractions With *not*

A **contraction** is two words made into one word. An **apostrophe** takes the place of the missing letter or letters. In a contraction, **not** becomes **n't**.

Read each sentence. Write a contraction for the underlined words.

 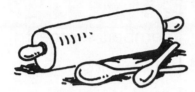 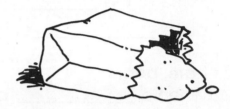

1. Cindy and Ed <u>could not</u> bake a cake. _____

2. There <u>was not</u> enough flour. _____

3. They <u>are not</u> happy _____

4. <u>Do not</u> give up! _____

5. They <u>did not</u> give up.
   They made cupcakes! _____

Write a sentence using a contraction you wrote.

_____

_____

# Chilly or Chili?

 **Homophones** *are words that sound the same but are spelled differently and have different meanings.*

Write the correct homophone in each blank to complete the sentences.

1. **bored, board**
   Some of the _____ members seemed

   quite _____ at the last meeting.

2. **bare, bear**
   When a _____ cub is born, it is _____,
   and its eyes are closed.

3. **chilly, chili**
   Nothing tastes better than a bowl of _____ on a _____ day.

4. **guest, guessed**
   Who would have _____ that your _____ was a thief!

5. **patients, patience**
   I wonder if doctors ever lose their _____ with difficult _____.

On another sheet of paper, rewrite each sentence using the correct homophones.

6. I'll meat you at ate inn the mourning.

7. Would ewe fix me sum tee and a bowl of serial?

8. My ant and uncle lived oversees four too years in Madrid.

9. Alex was sick with the flue and mist a hole weak of school.

10. I want two bye a knew pear of shoes, but I dew knot have a sent left.

Scholastic Teaching Resources  *Get Ready for 3rd Grade*

# A State Apart

The state of Michigan has two part—the Upper Peninsula and the Lower Peninsula. Peninsulas are long arms of land that jut into water. Both of Michigan's peninsulas are almost surrounded by the Great Lakes. The Upper Peninsula has many big forests. It is also rich in minerals. The Lower Peninsula has more people and large cities. Most of the state's industry is in the Lower Peninsula. Both peninsulas attract tourists who come to spend vacations in Michigan.

Read the paragraph. Add headings to the Venn diagram.
Then write facts in each part of the diagram.

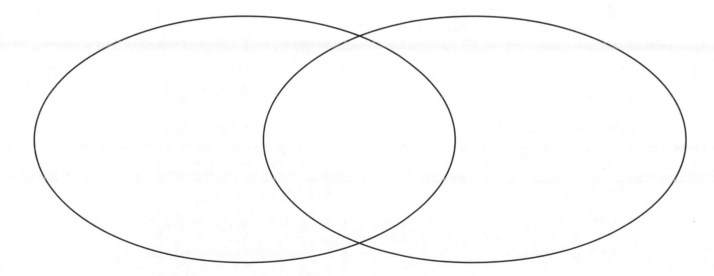

 **The Lower Peninsula of Michigan is larger in area than the Upper Peninsula. Add this fact to the diagram.**

# Garage Sale

Find and mark the ten spelling errors.

## We have grate stuff and big bargains!

### Office Supplys

- Big boxes of old newspaper

- Ballpoint pens that are out of ink

- Broken rubber bands

- Empty printer ink containers

### Clothing

- Singel left shoes

- Socks with hoales

- Jackets with broken zippers

- Sleeves that were cut off a shirt

### Household Goods

- Old phon books

- Torn sheets

- Old toothbrushes

- Empty pante cans

- Chipped plates

- A bunch of old pizza boxs

### Ferniture and Hardware

- A big box of bent nails

- A saggy bed

- A sofa with mice living in it

- A chare with only three legs

- A TV with only one channel

- Old dor knobs

Scholastic Teaching Resources   *Get Ready for 3rd Grade*

# Cow Code

HA HA HA HA
HA
HA

**Riddle: Where do cows go for entertainment?**

## What to Do

Find the corresponding numerals below. Then use the Decoder to solve the riddle by filling in the spaces at the bottom of the page. The first one has been done for you.

**Decoder**

| | |
|---|---|
| 23 | X |
| 17 | O |
| 153 | E |
| 21 | A |
| 370 | O |
| 108 | S |
| 76 | D |
| 9 | V |
| 15 | F |
| 67 | T |
| 22 | E |
| 435 | P |
| 86 | H |
| 88 | R |
| 45 | I |
| 534 | M |
| 118 | W |
| 543 | N |
| 307 | G |

1. nine                                         9   _____

2. twenty-two                            _____

3. seventeen                             _____

4. forty-five                               _____

5. sixty-seven                           _____

6. one hundred eight                _____

7. eighty-six                              _____

8. one hundred fifty-three        _____

9. three hundred seventy         _____

10. five hundred thirty-four       _____

**TO** __ __ __  " __ __ __ "  V __ __ __ __
    5  7  2    10 3 9   1 4 8 6

# Cake and Ice Cream

➡️ *Two sentences that share the same subject can be combined to make one sentence by using the word* and.

Rewrite the sentences by combining their endings.

1. The party was fun.
   The party was exciting.

   The party was fun and exciting.

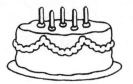

2. We blew up orange balloons.
   We blew up red balloons.

_____

3. We ate cake.
   We ate ice cream.

_____

4. The cake frosting was green.
   The cake frosting was yellow.

_____

5. We made a bookmark.
   We made a clay pot.

_____

6. We brought games.
   We brought prizes.

_____

Scholastic Teaching Resources   *Get Ready for 3rd Grade*

# Helping Your Child Get Ready: Week 6

These are the skills your child will be working on this week.

**Math**
- place value
- telling time

**Reading**
- comprehension
- compare/contrast

**Writing**
- building sentences

**Vocabulary**
- rhyming words

**Grammar**
- verbs
- pronouns
- adjectives

**Here are some activities you and your child might enjoy.**

**Mapping My World** Invite your child to draw pictures and write labels to make maps of familiar places, such as his or her school, a local park, or a favorite friend's home.

**Word Expert** Boost your child's vocabulary by playing Word Expert. Tell him or her that for each word you say, he or she must give you an antonym, a synonym, as well as an example of the word. For instance, if you say *exciting*, a synonym might be *thrilling*, an antonym might be *boring*, and an example could be *riding a rollercoaster*.

**Nutrition Label Math** Show examples of food labels to your child, ideally those with more than one serving in a package. Talk about what the numbers on the label mean. Then ask your child to determine the nutrition totals for the entire item. For example, if there are 2 servings in a small can of vegetables, your child can double the nutrition label numbers to find the total calories, fat and carbohydrate content, and so on.

**One-Minute Categories** Ask your child to name as many examples as possible of a category in one minute. For example, for animal, he or she might name dog, cat, wolf, tiger, and so on. Make the categories more challenging as his or skill increases. You can also specify naming an animal that starts with a particular letter. For example, for the letter *d*, animals would include dog, duck, and donkey.

**Your child might enjoy reading the following books.**

*Amber Brown Is Not a Crayon*
by Paula Danziger

*How to Be Cool in the Third Grade*
by Betsy Duffey

*Mice and Beans*
by Pam Muñoz Ryan

Letter D

dog, duck, donkey

_____ **'s Incentive Chart: Week 6**
Name Here

This week, I plan to read _____ minutes each day.

CHART YOUR PROGRESS HERE.

| Week 6 | Day 1 | Day 2 | Day 3 | Day 4 | Day 5 |
|---|---|---|---|---|---|
| I read for... | minutes | minutes | minutes | minutes | minutes |
| Put a sticker to show you completed each day's work. | | | | | |

# Congratulations!

Wow! You did a great job this week!

#1

Place sticker here.

**Parent or Caregiver's Signature** _____

# Cleaning the Alligator's Teeth

The alligator asked if I
Would clean his dirty teeth.
I climbed inside his jagged jaws
And brushed up underneath.

I felt his two jaws start to close.
His sharp teeth touched my skin.
I yelled, "I'm not a sandwich!
Open up and give a grin!"

The alligator laughed and made
His two jaws open wide.
I said, "The next time you do that
I'll have to pinch your hide."

He gave another 'gator laugh
That shook me head to toe.
I finished brushing all his teeth
And said, "I've got to go."

⭐ **SPECIAL WORDS** ⭐

| clean | jaws | start | grin | wide | stood |
|-------|------|-------|------|------|-------|

# Cleaning the Alligator's Teeth

## Reading Comprehension

Fill in the blanks with the word that best completes the sentence.

1. The alligator asked if I would brush his dirty _____ .

   claws          teeth          scales          tail

2. I climbed inside his jagged _____ .

   nose          ears          mouth          jaws

3. I felt his two jaws start to _____ .

   open          chew          lick          close

4. His _____ teeth touched my skin.

   many          white          sharp          mean

5. I yelled, "I'm not a sandwich, open up and give a

   _____ ."

   laugh          grin          yell          bite

## Rhyme Time

Circle the words in each column that rhyme with the word in bold. What other words rhyme with that word? Write them in the spaces below.

| **clean** | **jaws** | **start** | **grin** | **wide** | **stood** |
|-----------|----------|-----------|----------|----------|-----------|
| bean      | claws    | dart      | win      | wind     | good      |
| mean      | jam      | star      | fin      | hide     | stop      |
| seen      | laws     | cart      | pin      | ride     | hood      |

| _____ | _____ | _____ | _____ | _____ | _____ |
|----------|----------|----------|----------|----------|----------|
| _____ | _____ | _____ | _____ | _____ | _____ |

Scholastic Teaching Resources   *Get Ready for 3rd Grade*

# Colorful Fish

Look at the numbers in the shapes inside the fish.

Use the information in the key at right to color the shapes.

| If there is a . . . | Color the space . . . |
|---|---|
| 6 in the tens place | green |
| 5 in the hundreds place | blue |
| 2 in the ones place | yellow |
| 7 in the tens place | orange |
| 9 in the hundreds place | red |

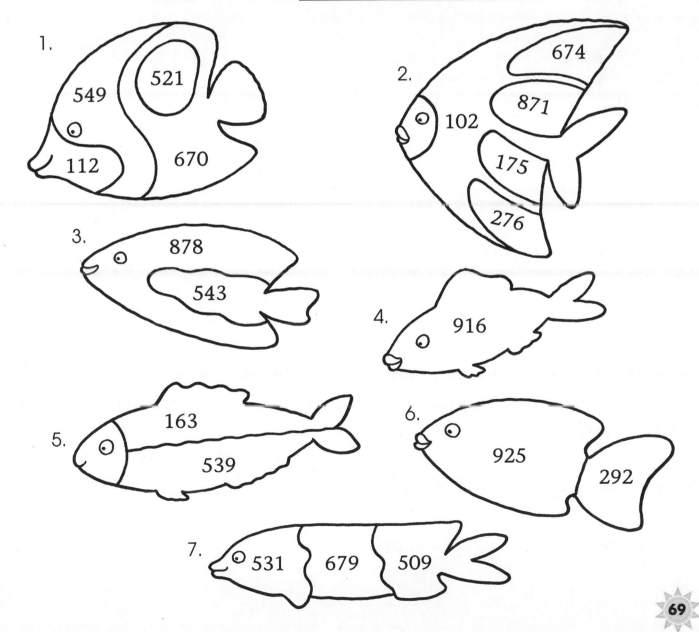

1. 549 521 112 670

2. 674 871 102 175 276

3. 878 543

4. 916

5. 163 539

6. 925 292

7. 531 679 509

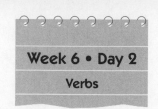

# Verbs *have*, *had*

The verb **have** is irregular. Use **have** or **has** to tell about the present. Use **had** to tell about the past.

Choose the correct word from the chart to complete each sentence.

| In the Present | In the Past |
| --- | --- |
| have, has | had |

1. Joe _____ new running shoes.

2. I _____ new shoes, too.

3. Last week we _____ old shoes.

4. I _____ a green shirt on.

5. Joe _____ a blue shirt on.

6. Yesterday we both _____ red shirts on.

7. Last year we _____ to walk to the park.

8. Now, I _____ skates.

9. Now, Joe _____ a bike.

**70**

# Get Your Ticket!

Write a sentence to match each picture. Be sure to include a subject, an action, and a part that tells where or when.

1. A boy climbs a tree in his backyard.

2. _____

3. _____

 **Find a cartoon in the newspaper. Use the pictures to write a sentence on another piece of paper. Be sure to include a subject, an action, and a part that tells where or when.**

# Slide Show

 *A sentence is more interesting when it includes a subject, an action, and a part that tells where or when.*

Write three sentences and draw pictures to match.

| subject | action | where or when |
|---------|--------|---------------|
|         |        |               |

1. _____

| subject | action | where or when |
|---------|--------|---------------|
|         |        |               |

2. _____

| subject | action | where or when |
|---------|--------|---------------|
|         |        |               |

3. _____

 **Switch the sentence parts around to make three silly sentences! Write the sentences on another piece of paper.**

# Play Ball

What's your favorite ball game? Many people like sports in which they throw a ball. In bowling and basketball, you throw a ball. Other people play games in which they hit a ball. Golf and tennis are two examples. Still another game in which a ball is hit is lacrosse. A third kind of ball game calls for kicking a ball. Players kick balls in soccer, football, rugby, and of course, kickball.

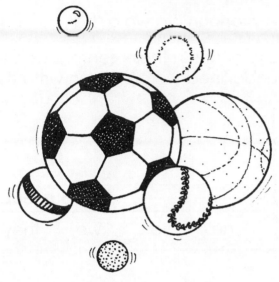

Read the paragraph. Then answer the questions.

1. What are four sports where you kick a ball? _____

2. What are three sports in which you hit a ball? _____

3. In what games do you throw a ball? _____

Use your answers to complete the chart.

| Hitting a Ball | Throwing a Ball | Kicking a Ball |
|---|---|---|
|  |  |  |

 **What do you do with the ball in baseball? Add baseball to the chart.**

73

# Send In the Subs

A **pronoun** is a word that can take the place of a noun.

The nouns in these sentences need a rest. Pick a pronoun to replace the underlined word(s). Then write the sentence with the pronoun.

| Pronoun Subs | | | | | |
|---|---|---|---|---|---|
| he | you | we | they | it | she |

1. <u>Tanya</u> swings the bat.

_____

2. <u>Mr. Bartlet and Mr. Jones</u> blow their whistles.

_____

3. <u>Matt and I</u> warm up.

_____

4. <u>Leo</u> looks for his glove.

_____

5. <u>The ball</u> rolls into the field.

_____

Check your sentences. Did you begin them with a capital letter?

Scholastic Teaching Resources  *Get Ready for 3rd Grade*

# Prime Timer

WRITE THE TIME 3 WAYS.

example:  ← 1:15
15 minutes after 1
45 minutes to 2

1. _____ _____

_____ minutes after _____

_____ minutes to _____

2. _____ _____

_____ minutes after _____

_____ minutes to _____

3. _____ _____

_____ minutes after _____

_____ minutes to _____

4. _____ _____

_____ minutes after _____

_____ minutes to _____

5. _____ _____

_____ minutes after _____

_____ minutes to _____

6. _____ _____

_____ minutes after _____

_____ minutes to _____

# Describing a Surprise

Use adjectives to describe an object.

Read the words on the box.
What do they describe?

_____

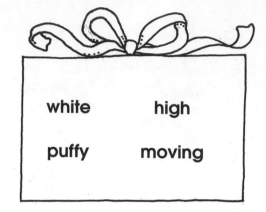

white        high

puffy       moving

Think of a surprise to hide in each box. Then write four adjectives to describe it.

1.

2.

3.

4.

Read your adjectives to a friend. Can your friend guess what the surprise is?
If not, can you think of better adjectives?

# Helping Your Child Get Ready: Week 7

These are the skills your child will be working on this week.

**Math**
- fractions
- using arrays

**Reading**
- comprehension
- compare/contrast
- cause and effect

**Writing**
- combining sentences
- verb usage

**Vocabulary**
- sight words/verbs
- prefixes/un-

**Grammar**
- sentence punctuation
- comparative/superlative

## Here are some activities you and your child might enjoy.

**Compliment Jar** Create a compliment jar by labeling a clear plastic jar with the word *Compliments*. Invite everyone in your home to write a compliment for another family member on a slip of paper and place it in the jar. Once a week, invite your child to read the compliments aloud to the rest of the family. For a twist, turn it into a guessing game. Your child can read the compliment but leave out the name. Can anyone guess this person's identity? Your child can provide clues, if necessary.

**List-en Up** Help your child develop good listening and memorization skills. Read a list of five items two times. Then ask your child to repeat the list back to you in order. Here is a list of the Great Lakes (in alphabetical order) to get your started: Lake Erie, Lake Huron, Lake Michigan, Lake Ontario, Lake Superior

**Character Friends** Ask your child to talk about a character in one of the books he or she has been reading. You can prompt the discussion by asking questions like these: *Which characters would you want to be friends with in real life? What are some of the good qualities this character has? How are you and the character similar or different?*

**Summer Games** Plan a mini "Summer Olympics" with your family. Play classic picnic games such as a water-balloon toss or a three-legged race, or make up fun games of your own. Take turns trying them!

## Your child might enjoy reading the following books.

*American Tall Tales*
by Mary Pope Osborne

*In the Year of the Boar and Jackie Robinson*
by Betty Bao Lord

*Tiger Math: Learning to Graph From a Baby Tiger*
by Ann Whitehead Nagda

_____ **'s Incentive Chart: Week 7**

This week, I plan to read _____ minutes each day.

CHART YOUR PROGRESS HERE.

| **Week 7** | Day 1 | Day 2 | Day 3 | Day 4 | Day 5 |
|---|---|---|---|---|---|
|  **I read for...** | minutes | minutes | minutes | minutes | minutes |
| Put a sticker to show you completed each day's work. | | | | | |

# Congratulations!

Wow! You did a great job this week!

Place sticker here.

**Parent or Caregiver's Signature** _____

# Fraction Fun

Something that is split in 2 equal parts is divided in "half."

These two shapes are divided in half.

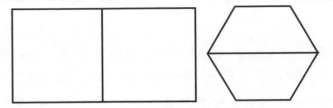

A fraction has a number on the top: ⟶ 1

A fraction has a number on the bottom, too: ⟶ 2

The top number tells the "fraction," or parts, of the whole.

The bottom number tells the number of parts in the whole.

A. **Draw a line to match the picture with a fraction.**

$\dfrac{2}{2}$    $\dfrac{2}{12}$    $\dfrac{2}{3}$

B. **The top number in these fractions tells you how many parts to color. Try it!**

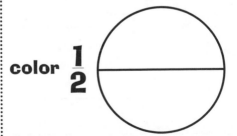

color $\dfrac{1}{2}$

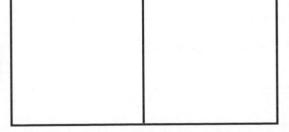

color $\dfrac{2}{2}$

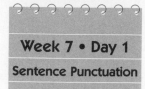
# Statements and Questions

A **statement** is a sentence that tells something. It ends with a period. A **question** is a sentence that asks something. It ends with a question mark.

A. Read each sentence. Write Q on the line if the sentence is a question. Write S if the sentence is a statement.

1. Where did the ant live?　　　　　————

2. The ant had many cousins.　　　　————

3. She found the crumb under a leaf.　————

4. How will she carry it?　　　　　　————

5. Who came along first?　　　　　　————

6. The lizard wouldn't help.　　　　　————

7. He said he was too cold.　　　　　————

8. Why did the rooster fly away?　　　————

B. The sentences below do not make sense. Rewrite the words in the correct order.

1. How crumb did carry the ant the?

　————————————————————

　————————————————————

2. She herself it carried.

　————————————————————

　————————————————————

Scholastic Teaching Resources  *Get Ready for 3rd Grade*

# Blending In

How are the following words alike: *blue, black, blink*? If you said they all begin with *bl*, you're right. Some other words that begin with these letters are *blob, blanket,* and *blimp*. Letter pairs like *bl* are blends. Blends are two or more consonants that work together. What blend do the following words begin with: *green, gray, grumpy*? Two other blends are *tr* and *sm*. Words such as *smoke, smile, try, tray, smack, trick, truck,* and *smell* begin with these blends.

Use the paragraph to write four headings for the chart. Then write examples under each heading.

| | | | |
|---|---|---|---|
| | | | |

 **Add at least two more words to each group on the chart.**

# Great Gardening Tips

Sentences can also be combined to make them more interesting. Key words can help put two sentences together.

**I will plan my garden. I am waiting for spring.**

**I will plan my garden while I am waiting for spring.**

Combine the two sentences using the key word. Write a new sentence.

1. Fill a cup with water. Add some flower seeds.  and

_____

2. This will soften the seeds. They are hard.  because

_____

3. Fill a cup with dirt. The seeds soak in water.  while

_____

4. Bury the seeds in the cup. The dirt covers them.  until

_____

5. Add water to the plant. Do not add too much.  but

_____

6. Set the cup in the sun. The plant will grow.  so

_____

Scholastic Teaching Resources   *Get Ready for 3rd Grade*

# A-maze-ing Verbs

To complete the maze, pass only through the correct sentences. An incorrect sentence is like a wall in the maze: You cannot pass through it. The correct path takes you through nine boxes.

start

Lilly **drew** a picture.

I **talks** a lot.

Sam **held** his nose.

Lilly **draw** a picture.

Jake and Sam **buys** candy.

Jake and Sam **writes** stories.

Lilly **thinked** Sam was nice.

Jake **thought** hard.

Sam **wrote** a letter.

Jake **bought** some candy.

Lilly **brought** Pete to school.

Yesterday, Lilly **bring** Pete to school.

Jake **laughed** at Sam's joke.

Lilly and Pete **walked** home.

Sam **hurted** his toe.

Finish

My head **hurts.**

# Three Nests

You can use **adjectives** to compare things. To compare two things, add **-er** to the adjective. To compare three or more things, add **-est.**

Biddie Bird has a friend named Betty. Betty always wants to outdo Biddie. If Biddie has a clean nest, Betty has a cleaner nest. Biddie and Betty have another friend named Birdie. She likes to outdo both Biddie and Betty. So she has the cleanest nest.

Read the sentences. Then fill in the chart so the correct form of each adjective is under each bird's name.

| Biddie | Betty | Birdie |
|---|---|---|
| clean | cleaner | cleanest |
| 1. _____ | _____ | _____ |
| 2. _____ | _____ | _____ |
| 3. _____ | _____ | _____ |
| 4. _____ | _____ | _____ |
| 5. _____ | _____ | _____ |
| 6. _____ | _____ | _____ |

1. Betty's nest is <u>newer</u> than Biddie's.

2. Biddie has a <u>small</u> nest.

3. Birdie has the <u>warmest</u> nest of all.

4. Biddie's nest is <u>round</u>.

5. Birdie built the <u>neatest</u> nest.

6. Betty has a <u>softer</u> nest than Biddie.

Use the words you wrote on the chart to draw a picture of each bird's nest.

Scholastic Teaching Resources  *Get Ready for 3rd Grade*

# Fool the Birds

A woman in Virginia had a problem. Birds ate all the seeds she carefully planted. The woman put brown belts along the newly planted rows in her garden. Just as she had hoped, the birds thought the belts were snakes! As a result, the birds stayed out of the garden. The woman's plants grew in peace.

Read the paragraph. Then complete the cause-and-effect map.

**Other Effects**

**Cause**

**First Effect**

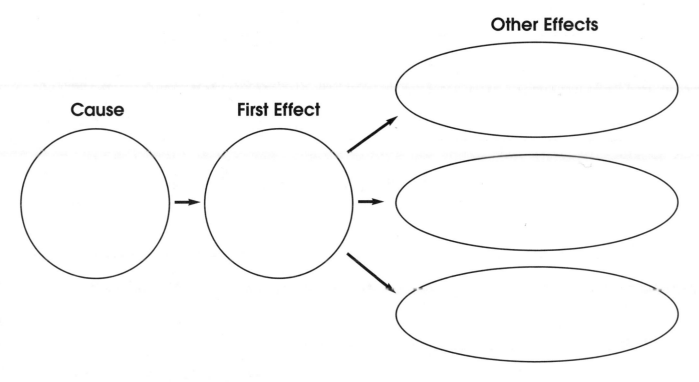

 **MORE!** What conclusions can you make about birds and snakes?

# Banana-Rama

Color the word that is missing from each sentence.

1. We _____ a spelling test yesterday. taked    took

2. There _____ frost on the ground. was    were

3. Tommy _____ the Statue of Liberty. seen    saw

4. How _____ elephants are at the zoo? much    many

5. Carla _____ her lizard to school. brought    brang

6. Have you _____ my dog? seen    saw

7. Alyssa _____ a new pair of skates. gots    has

8. You _____ supposed to finish your work. are    is

9. We _____ standing near a snake! were    was

10. They _____ a pig in the mud. seen    saw

11. We _____ our winter boots. wore    weared

12. Is she _____ to come over? gonna    going

13. _____ your cat climb trees? Do    Does

14. Rosie _____ cookies to the bake sale. brang    brought

Scholastic Teaching Resources  Get Ready for 3rd Grade

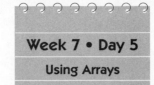
# A Ray of Fun

 An **array** demonstrates a multiplication sentence. The first **factor** tells how many rows there are. The second **factor** tells how many there are in each row. The answer of a multiplication sentence is called the **product**.

2 x 4 = 8     O O O O     2 rows
              O O O O     4 in each row

Write the multiplication sentence for each array.

A.  O O O
    O O O

_____

B.  O O O
    O O O
    O O O

_____

C.  O O
    O O
    O O
    O O

_____

D.  O O O O O
    O O O O O
    O O O O O

_____

E.  O O O

_____

F.  O O O
    O O O
    O O O
    O O O

_____

G.  O O O O O O
    O O O O O O

_____

H.  O O O O
    O O O O
    O O O O

_____

I.  O O O O O O
    O O O O O O
    O O O O O O

_____

J.  O O O
    O O O
    O O O
    O O O
    O O O

_____

K.  O
    O
    O
    O

_____

L.  O O
    O O
    O O
    O O
    O O
    O O

_____

 **It was time for our family photo. The photographer arranged us into four rows. There were six people in each row. How many people in all were in the photo? On another piece of paper, draw an array to solve this problem.**

# How Unusual!

The prefix **un-** means either "not" or "do the opposite of" in each word below. Circle each base word in the puzzle. The words go →, ↓, ↗, and ↘.

| | | | | | |
|---|---|---|---|---|---|
| unpack | untie | unload | unlock | unwind | undo |
| unknown | unfold | unable | unfair | unusual | unwise |

| | | | | | | | | |
|---|---|---|---|---|---|---|---|---|
| R | A | I | L | I | M | A | F | X |
| N | E | E | O | F | F | O | L | D |
| I | W | E | A | W | A | X | L | E |
| A | I | X | D | L | I | I | O | T |
| T | S | K | N | O | W | N | R | N |
| R | E | V | O | C | Z | R | D | I |
| E | P | A | C | K | X | E | A | A |
| C | A | B | L | E | S | Y | Z | P |
| D | N | I | K | U | S | U | A | L |

Write a word from the list to complete each sentence.

1. It is _____ for James to be late for school.

2. It took me ten minutes to _____ the knot.

3. You need a key to _____ the trunk.

4. We grew more concerned as the story began to _____.

5. It is _____ to wait until the last minute to do your homework.

6. Bill thought the umpire's call was _____.

Scholastic Teaching Resources *Get Ready for 3rd Grade*

# Helping Your Child Get Ready: Week 8

These are the skills your child will be working on this week.

**Math**
- fractions
- multiplication

**Reading**
- finding the main idea
- reading for details
- comprehension

**Vocabulary**
- proofreading/spelling
- sight words

**Writing**
- sequencing
- commas

**Grammar**
- singular and plural nouns
- sentence types

**Here are some activities you and your child might enjoy.**

**Spinning Stories** Cut out ten pictures from a magazine. Put them in a bag. Invite your child to take them out two or three at a time and use the pictures to tell a story.

**20 Questions** This favorite game can be used to build thinking skills. First choose a category, such as animal. Then think of one animal. Tell your child that he or she can ask only "yes" or "no" questions to determine the animal you are thinking of. Once he or she gets the hang of it, take turns asking questions.

**Going Acrostic** Provide opportunities for your child to create "acrostic" poems. To begin an acrostic poem, first write any word vertically (you may wish to start with your child's name). Then your child, going from top to bottom, uses each letter of the word as the first letter in another word—one that relates to the original word—and writes that word horizontally.

**Food Fractions** Fractions are fun to practice using foods like pizza or various fruits. With your child, define the whole item. Then divide it in half, quarters, eighths, or more. What is the smallest piece you can make?

**Your child might enjoy reading the following books.**

*Charlotte's Web*
by E.B. White

*The Mouse and the Motorcycle*
by Beverly Cleary

*The Wright Brothers at Kitty Hawk*
by Donald J. Sobol

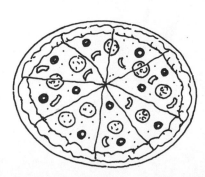

_____ 's Incentive Chart: Week 8

Name Here

This week, I plan to read _____ minutes each day.

CHART YOUR PROGRESS HERE.

| Week 8 | Day 1 | Day 2 | Day 3 | Day 4 | Day 5 |
|---|---|---|---|---|---|
| I read for... | minutes | minutes | minutes | minutes | minutes |
| Put a sticker to show you completed each day's work. | | | | | |

# Congratulations!

Wow! You did a great job this week!

#1

Place sticker here.

Parent or Caregiver's Signature _____

# How to "Ride" a Poem

Find and mark the ten spelling errors.

Writeing a poem

Is like riding a bike

Once you start riding

You ride where you like.

For exampel, I can write

Any wurd I want here

As long as it rhymes

And soundes good to the ear.

I can write in any style

I can write in any spede

As long as my readrs

Continue to read.

There'is only one danger

One risk that I run

When I sense that my readers

Have stoped having fun.

At this point its' best

Not to delay

Simply kick up your kickstand

And just ride eway.

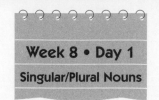

# One, or More

A **singular noun** names one person, place, or thing. A **plural noun** names more than one person, place, or thing. Add **-s** to form the plural of most nouns.

A.  Each sentence has an underlined noun. On the line, write S if it is a singular noun. Write P if it is a plural noun.

1. She has a new <u>baby</u>.                    _____

2. <u>It</u> is very cute.                              _____

3. She has small <u>fingers</u>.               _____

4. She drinks from a <u>bottle</u>.          _____

5. I can tell my <u>friends</u> all about it.   _____

B.  Read each sentence. Underline the singular noun. Circle the plural noun.

1. The baby has two sisters.

2. The nightgown has pockets.

3. Her hand has tiny fingers.

4. My parents have a baby.

5. The family has three girls.

C.  Complete the chart. Write the singular or plural of each noun.

| Singular | Plural |
|----------|--------|
| fence |  |
|  | trains |
| gate |  |
|  | cows |

Scholastic Teaching Resources    *Get Ready for 3rd Grade*

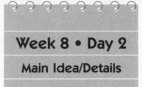

# The Milky Way

 The **main idea** of a story tells what the story is mostly about. **Details** in a story tell more information about the main idea.

What do you think of when you hear the words, "Milky Way?" Do you think of a candy bar? Well, there is another Milky Way, and you live in it! It is our galaxy. A galaxy is a grouping of stars. Scientists have learned that there are many galaxies in outer space. The Milky Way is a spiral-shaped galaxy with swirls of stars spinning out from the center of it. Scientists believe there are about 200 billion stars in the Milky Way. In this galaxy, nine planets orbit the sun. One of them is Earth. Even from Earth, on a clear night away from city lights, you can see part of the Milky Way. It is called that because so many stars close together look like a milky white stripe across the sky. However, if you looked at it with a telescope, you would see that it is made up of thousands of stars.

**Complete the main idea and each detail about the story.**

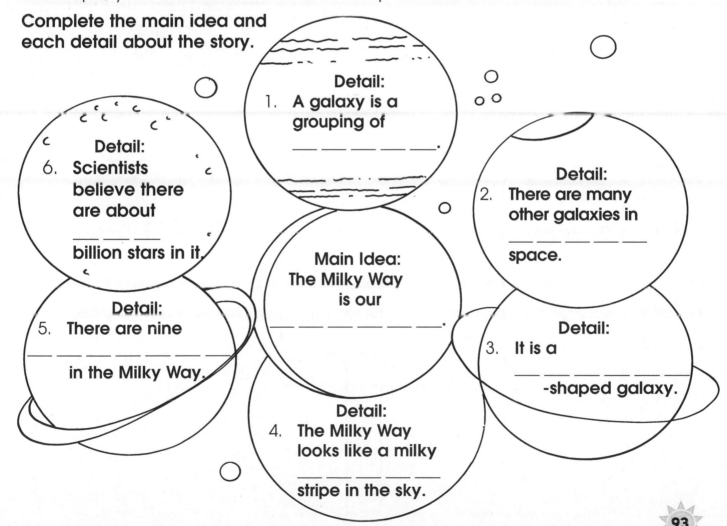

Detail:
1. A galaxy is a grouping of
   _ _ _ _ _ _ _ .

Detail:
6. Scientists believe there are about
   _ _ _ _
   billion stars in it.

Detail:
2. There are many other galaxies in
   _ _ _ _ _ _
   space.

Main Idea:
The Milky Way is our
_ _ _ _ _ _ .

Detail:
5. There are nine
   _ _ _ _ _ _ _
   in the Milky Way.

Detail:
3. It is a
   _ _ _ _ _ _
   -shaped galaxy.

Detail:
4. The Milky Way looks like a milky
   _ _ _ _ _
   stripe in the sky.

# Puzzle It Out!

Use the words in the Word Box to complete the sentences below.
Then write the words in the correct spaces in the puzzle.

**Across**

1. My name was the first

   _____ that I learned to spell.

3. Sam washed the dishes so they were

   sparkling _____ .

4. The weather today is _____

   but not hot.

5. At the end of second grade, our

   teacher said we were _____

   for third.

**Down**

2. Will you share my popcorn, or do

   you want your _____?

3. She has to _____ the baby

   because he's too little to walk.

6. We had burgers for dinner last

   night, and we're having them

   _____ tonight.

## Word Box

| | |
|---|---|
| carry | warm |
| own | clean |
| again | word |
| ready | |

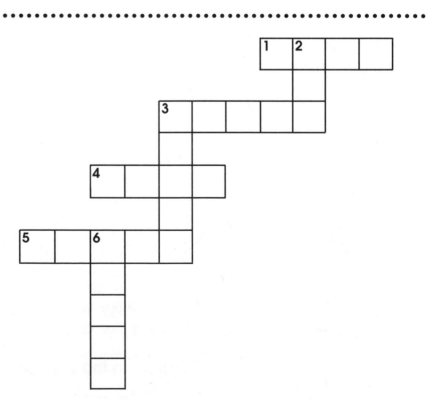

Scholastic Teaching Resources    *Get Ready for 3rd Grade*

# More Fun With Fractions

A fraction has two numbers. The top number will tell you how many parts to color. The bottom number tells you how many total parts there are.

A. $\frac{10}{10}$ is the whole circle.

Color $\frac{8}{10}$ of the circle.

How much is not colored? ___

B. $\frac{10}{10}$ is the whole rectangle.

Color $\frac{4}{10}$ of the rectangle.

How much is not colored? ___

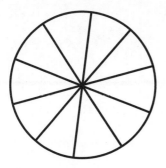

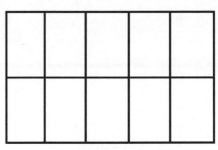

$$\frac{10}{10} - \frac{8}{10} = \underline{\phantom{-}}$$

$$\frac{10}{10} - \frac{4}{10} = \underline{\phantom{-}}$$

C. Solve this fraction equation. Cross out the dogs to help you.

$$\frac{10}{10} - \frac{3}{10} = \underline{\phantom{-}}$$

# Exclamations and Commands

An **exclamation** is a sentence that shows strong feeling. It ends with an exclamation point. A **command** is a sentence that gives an order. It ends with a period.

A. Read each sentence. Write E on the line if the sentence is an exclamation. Write C if the sentence is a command.

1. They chase buffaloes! _____

2. You have to go, too. _____

3. Wait at the airport. _____

4. It snows all the time! _____

5. Alligators live in the sewers! _____

6. Look at the horse. _____

7. That's a great-looking horse! _____

8. Write a letter to Seymour. _____

B. Complete each exclamation and command. The punctuation mark at the end of each line is a clue.

1. I feel _____!

2. Help your _____.

3. That's a _____!

4. I lost _____!

5. Turn the _____.

6. Come watch the _____.

7. Please let me _____.

Scholastic Teaching Resources  *Get Ready for 3rd Grade*

# Lulu to the Rescue

| **VOLUME X** | Anyplace, USA | **Monday, June 11** |
|---|---|---|

JoAnne Altsman always thought her pet pig LuLu was a good companion. Now she also thinks of LuLu as a hero. Why? When JoAnne suffered a heart attack in 1998, LuLu saved her life.

JoAnne was vacationing in her camper when she fell ill. She yelled for help, but no one heard her cries. LuLu knew that JoAnne was in trouble. She pushed through a dog door and ran to the road. She tried to stop passing cars but had no luck. LuLu hurried back to the camper three times to see how JoAnne was.

At last LuLu did something drivers were sure to notice. She lay down on the road and stuck her feet in the air. Finally, a car stopped. The driver got out and followed LuLu back to the camper. JoAnne heard the man knocking on the door. "There's something wrong with your pig!" he yelled.

"There's something wrong with me!" JoAnne yelled back. "Call 911!"

Before long, help was on its way. Today JoAnne is well, and she's grateful for her pet pig. Without LuLu, she would have died.

1. Where was JoAnne when she fell ill?
   A. on vacation
   B. at school
   C. in her home
   D. at work

2. Why did LuLu push her way out of the camper and run to the road?

   _____

3. "LuLu was a good companion." What is a companion?
   F. guard
   G. nurse
   H. doctor
   J. friend

4. What probably happened after the man knocked on the door of the camper? Tell two things that probably happened.

   _____

   _____

# Stories of Nature

 *Sentences should be written in the correct order to tell a story.*

Finish the stories by writing a sentence about each of the last two pictures.

 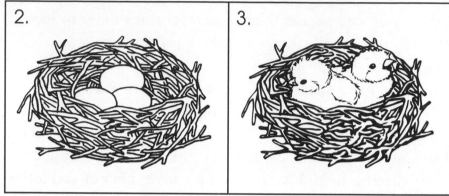

**First: Two birds build a nest.**

**Next:** _____

**Last:** _____

**First: A flower bud grows.**

**Next:** _____

**Last:** _____

Scholastic Teaching Resources   *Get Ready for 3rd Grade*

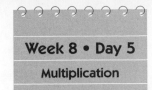
# Time to Group

 *The multiplication symbol (x) can be thought of as meaning "groups of."*

3 "groups of" 4 equals 12
3 x 4 = 12

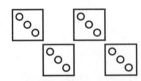

5 "groups of" 2 equals 10.
5 x 2 = 10

## Write the multiplication sentence for each diagram.

A.    B.    C. 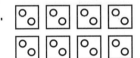   D.

_____   _____   _____   _____

E. 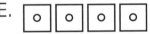   F.    G. 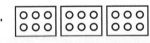   H.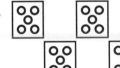

_____   _____   _____   _____

I.    J.    K. 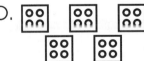   L.

_____   _____   _____   _____

M.    N.   O.   P.

_____   _____   _____   _____

 **William has five bags of hamburgers. There are seven hamburgers in each bag. On another piece of paper, show the total number of hamburgers.**

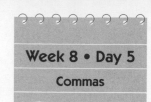

# The Sky's the Limit

➡️ *Some sentences include a list. A **comma** (,) is used to separate each item in the list.*

*For example:* Mrs. Jones asked the class to work on pages two, three, and four.

Fill in the blanks to make a list in each sentence. Watch for commas!

1. I ate _____, _____,

   and _____ for breakfast.

2. We stayed with Grandma on _____,

   _____, and _____ nights.

3. I found _____, _____,

   and _____ in my party bag.

4. The boys played _____,

   _____, and _____

   at summer camp.

5. The _____, _____,

   and _____ ate the corn we scattered.

6. The pigs built their houses using _____,

   _____, and _____.

 **Cut a balloon out of paper. On one side, list three objects that fly. On the other side, write a sentence that lists the objects shown on the right side of this page.**

Scholastic Teaching Resources  *Get Ready for 3rd Grade*

# Helping Your Child Get Ready: Week 9

These are the skills your child will be working on this week.

## Math
- multiplication
- bar graph

## Reading
- sequencing
- following directions

## Writing
- proofreading
- sentence fragments

## Vocabulary
- word relationships
- common phrases

## Grammar
- common and proper nouns
- adjectives

**Here are some activities you and your child might enjoy.**

**Math in a Menu** When you and your child are looking at a menu, take the opportunity to practice math concepts. Ask questions like these: *Which food item costs the most? How much is it? Which item costs the least? If you bought the most expensive and the least expensive items, how much would you spend altogether?*

**Summer Fun With A–Z** Ask your child to think about what he or she loves about summer. Then challenge him or her to write about these things in sentences that use all 26 letters of the alphabet. Encourage your child to circle each letter the first time it is used.

**Double Meanings** Reinforce the concept of homonyms with your child by challenging him or her to find two (or more!) meanings for each of these words: bob, fair, lock, pitcher.

**How Puzzling!** Invite your child to create a jigsaw puzzle Provide a large piece of paper, crayons or colored markers, and scissors. First your child can draw a picture. Then he or she can cut it up into smaller pieces and mix them up. See if you, or another family member can put it back together!

**Your child might enjoy reading the following books.**

*Charlie and the Chocolate Factory*
by Roald Dahl

*So You Want to Be President?*
by Judith St. George

*Tea With Milk*
by Allen Say

_____ **'s Incentive Chart: Week 9**
Name Here

This week, I plan to read _____ minutes each day.

CHART YOUR PROGRESS HERE.

| Week 9 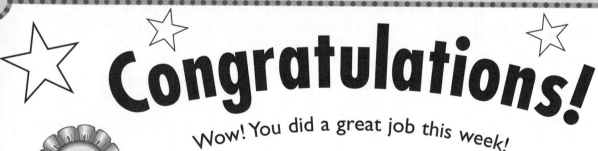 | Day 1 | Day 2 | Day 3 | Day 4 | Day 5 |
|---|---|---|---|---|---|
| I read for... | minutes | minutes | minutes | minutes | minutes |
| Put a sticker to show you completed each day's work. | ⭕ ⭕ | ⭕ ⭕ | ⭕ ⭕ | ⭕ ⭕ | ⭕ ⭕ |

# Congratulations!

Wow! You did a great job this week!

Place sticker here.

**Parent or Caregiver's Signature** _____

# The Father of Our Country

 *After you finish reading, go back and look for mistakes.*

Use the proofreading marks to correct eight mistakes in the letter.

<u>mars</u> = **Make a capital letter.**     ( ? ) = **Add a question mark.**     ( ! ) = **Add an exclamation point.**

( · ) = **Add a period.**     ( , ) = **Add a comma.**

> Dear Friend,
>
> my job as the first president of the United States was hard  My friends and I had to make new laws new money, and new jobs. the capital was in New York when I became president. then it moved to Philadelphia. Is the capital still there. Who is the president today! I would love to see how the United States has changed over the past two hundred years?
>
> Sincerely,
>
> George Washington

 **On another piece of paper, write a letter to today's president. The White House address is: 1600 Pennsylvania Avenue, Washington, D.C. 20500.**

# Adding Quickly

*The addition sentence 4 + 4 + 4 + 4 + 4 = 20 can be written as a multiplication sentence. Count how many times 4 is being added together. The answer is 5. So, 4 + 4 + 4 + 4 + 4 = 20 can be written as 5 x 4 = 20. Multiplication is a quick way to add.*

Write a multiplication sentence for each addition sentence.

A.  5 + 5 + 5 = 15

_____

B.  6 + 6 + 6 + 6 = 24

_____

C.  8 + 8 = 16

_____

D.  2 + 2 + 2 + 2 = 8

_____

E.  7 + 7 + 7 = 21

_____

F.  4 + 4 + 4 + 4 = 16

_____

G.  9 + 9 + 9 = 27

_____

H.  5 + 5 + 5 + 5 + 5 = 25

_____

I.  3 + 3 + 3 + 3 + 3 = 15

_____

J.  10 + 10 + 10 + 10 = 40

_____

K.  1 + 1 + 1 + 1 + 1 = 5

_____

L.  11 + 11 + 11 = 33

_____

M.  8 + 8 + 8 + 8 = 32

_____

N.  0 + 0 + 0 + 0 = 0

_____

O.  12 + 12 + 12 + 12 = 48

_____

P.  9 + 9 + 9 + 9 = 36

_____

**Today, we are going to the beach. Mom packed the picnic basket with six sandwiches, six water bottles, six candy bars, and six apples. How many items did she pack in all?**

Scholastic Teaching Resources    Get Ready for 3rd Grade

# Common or Proper?

A **common noun** names any person, place, or thing. A **proper noun** names a particular person, place, or thing. A proper noun begins with a capital letter.

A. Is the underlined word a common noun or a proper noun?
Write *common* or *proper*.

1. The <u>girl</u> likes to learn. _____

2. She goes to two <u>schools</u>. _____

3. She lives in <u>America</u>. _____

B. Underline the common nouns. Circle the proper nouns.

1. April has a brother and a sister.

2. Their names are Julius and May.

3. Their parents were born in Taiwan.

4. April goes to school on Saturday.

5. She is learning a language called Mandarin.

6. May read a book about the Middle Ages.

C. Underline the common nouns. Circle the proper nouns.
Then write them on the chart in the correct category.

1. Last August David went to camp.

2. Many children go to a picnic on the Fourth of July.

| Common Nouns | Proper Nouns |
|---|---|
| _____ | _____ |
| _____ | _____ |
| _____ | _____ |

# Dinnertime

A **sentence** is a group of words that expresses a complete thought.
A **fragment** is an incomplete thought.

Write S for sentence or F for fragment.

_____ 1. Insects eat many different things.

_____ 2. Some of these things.

_____ 3. The praying mantis eats other insects.

_____ 4. Water bugs eat tadpoles and small frogs.

_____ 5. Flower nectar makes good.

_____ 6. Build nests to store their food.

_____ 7. The cockroach will eat almost anything.

_____ 8. Termites.

_____ 9. A butterfly caterpillar.

_____ 10. Bite animals and people.

_____ 11. Some insects will even eat paper.

_____ 12. Insects have different mouth parts to help them eat.

**On another piece of paper, write about three things you did during the day using only sentence fragments. Have someone read it. Did they understand it? Why or why not?**

Scholastic Teaching Resources  *Get Ready for 3rd Grade*

# Scrambled Eggs

 **Sequencing** *means putting the events of a story in the order in which they happened.*

**The sentences below are scrambled. Number them in the correct sequence.**

A. ____ I took a shower.
____ I got out of bed.
____ I got dressed.

B. ____ She planted the seeds.
____ Big pink flowers bloomed.
____ Tiny green shoots came up.

C. ____ He ate the sandwich.
____ He spread some jelly on them.
____ He got out two pieces of bread.

D. ____ He slid down the slide.
____ He climbed up the ladder.
____ He landed on his feet.

E. ____ We built a snowman.
____ Low gray clouds drifted in.
____ It began to snow hard.

F. ____ Firefighters put out the fire.
____ Lightning struck the barn.
____ The barn caught on fire.

G. ____ The pepper spilled out of the jar.
____ I sneezed.
____ My nose began to itch.

H. ____ "My name is Emma."
____ "Hi, what is your name?"
____ "It's nice to meet you, Emma."

I. ____ I said, "Okay, do a trick first."
____ Rover whined for a treat.
____ I gave him a dog biscuit.
____ He danced on his hind legs.

J. ____ She built a nest.
____ Baby birds hatched from the eggs.
____ I saw a robin gathering straw.
____ She laid four blue eggs.

# Adjectives

An **adjective** is a word that describes a person, place, or thing.

A. Read each sentence. Write the adjective that describes the underlined noun on the line.

1. We live near a sparkling <u>brook</u>. _____

2. It has clear <u>water</u>. _____

3. Large <u>fish</u> swim in the brook. _____

4. Busy <u>squirrels</u> play near the brook. _____

5. You can enjoy breathing in the fresh <u>air</u> near the brook. _____

B. Complete each sentence by adding an adjective.

1. I love _____ apples.

2. I see a _____ ball.

3. I smell _____ flowers.

4. I hear _____ music.

5. I like the _____ taste of pickles.

 **Write three sentences that tell about the foods you like the best. Use adjectives in your description.**

Scholastic Teaching Resources  *Get Ready for 3rd Grade*

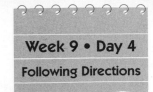
# Sneaky Snakes

Snakes are very good at hiding. Most snakes can **camouflage** themselves into their environment. That means they have different colors and patterns on their bodies that allow them to blend in with the colors and patterns of things around them. Camouflage helps them hide from their enemies and helps them be **sneaky** when they are trying to capture something to eat. For example, the emerald tree boa lives in the **jungle**. Its green skin makes it nearly invisible among the green leaves of the trees. **Rattlesnakes** live in rocky, dry places. The patterns of black, tan, and brown on their backs help them blend in with their rocky environment. The horned viper lives in the desert. Its skin is the same color as **sand** where it burrows underground. It is hard to see unless it is moving. Also, some snakes that are harmless look very similar to **venomous** snakes. The harmless milk snake is colored orange, with yellow and black stripes, much like the poisonous **coral snake**. The enemies of the milk snake mistake it for a coral snake because they look so much alike.

**Find the answers in the story. Write them in the puzzle.**

1. Write the word that starts with a v and means "poisonous."

2. Write another word for "tricky."

3. Write what helps a snake blend in with its surroundings.

4. Write where emerald tree boas live.

5. Write what snakes live in rocky places and have black, tan, and brown patterned skin.

6. Write what is the same color as the horned viper.

7. Write the name of the snake that looks like a milk snake.

Write the letter from the numbered squares in the puzzle above to fill in each box.

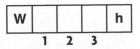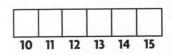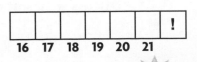

Scholastic Teaching Resources    Get Ready for 3rd Grade

# How It Is

Circle the correct word to complete each sentence.

1. An ant is black, and a grasshopper is _____.
   A. blue          B. fuzzy          C. green

2. A shirt is cotton, and a jar is _____.
   A. glass          B. silk          C. jam

3. A hill is rolling, and a river is _____.
   A. winding          B. rainy          C. steep

4. A daisy is white, and a rose is _____.
   A. green          B. dirty          C. red

5. A ring is round, and a box is _____.
   A. wool          B. square          C. happy

6. An elephant is large, and a mouse is _____.
   A. small          B. huge          C. yellow

7. A puddle is muddy, and a pool is _____.
   A. sad          B. clear          C. shy

8. A hammer is hard, and a pillow is _____.
   A. sleepy          B. sharp          C. soft

 **Discuss with someone why you did not choose the other words.**

Scholastic Teaching Resources   *Get Ready for 3rd Grade*

# "Fun and Games"

 *Some words like "hammer and nails" and "salt and pepper" just go together.*

Choose a word from the box to complete each phrase.

| | |
|---|---|
| sooner | right |
| chips | sweet |
| order | lost |
| sugar | effect |
| bacon | fun |
| shine | business |
| error | easy |
| name | gentlemen |
| cup | alive |
| cents | pots |

1. cause and _____

2. _____ and games

3. _____ and saucer

4. cream and _____

5. _____ and found

6. _____ and address

7. ladies and _____

8. law and _____

9. _____ and sour

10. nice and _____

11. trial and _____

12. _____ and pans

13. fish and _____

14. rain or _____

15. _____ or pleasure

16. _____ or wrong

17. dead or _____

18. dollars and _____

19. _____ and eggs

20. _____ or later

 **On another sheet of paper, list three other pairs of words that go together.**

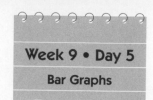

# Great Graphing

A. How many pennies equal 5¢? Color in the boxes on the graph to show your answer. How many nickels equal 5¢? Color in the boxes on the graph to show your answer.

| | 1 | 2 | 3 | 4 | 5 | 6 | 7 | 8 | 9 | 10 |
|---|---|---|---|---|---|---|---|---|---|---|
| **Pennies** | | | | | | | | | | |
| **Nickels** | | | | | | | | | | |

B. How many pennies equal 10¢? Color in the boxes on the graph to show your answer. How many nickels equal 10¢? Color in the boxes on the graph to show your answer. How many dimes equal 10¢? Color in the boxes on the graph to show your answer.

| | 1 | 2 | 3 | 4 | 5 | 6 | 7 | 8 | 9 | 10 |
|---|---|---|---|---|---|---|---|---|---|---|
| **Pennies** | | | | | | | | | | |
| **Nickels** | | | | | | | | | | |
| **Dimes** | | | | | | | | | | |

C. How many pennies equal 25¢? Color in the boxes on the graph to show your answer. How many nickels equal 25¢? Color in the boxes on the graph to show your answer. How many quarters equal 25¢? Color in the boxes on the graph to show your answer.

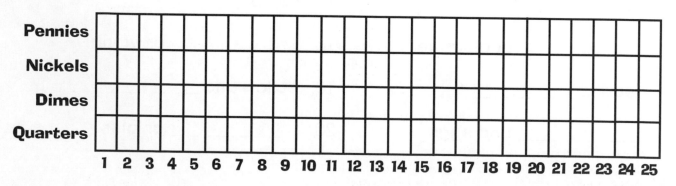

# Helping Your Child Get Ready: Week 10

These are the skills your child will be working on this week.

**Math**
- division
- geometric shapes

**Reading**
- cause and effect

**Writing**
- punctuating questions

**Vocabulary**
- antonyms
- compound words

**Grammar**
- adjectives
- possessives
- prepositions

**Here are some activities you and your child might enjoy.**

**Snappy Summaries** Writing a summary is often hard for children. To help your child sharpen this important skill, have him or her create one-sentence summaries of favorite books, movies, or television shows. To do this, have your child answer this question: *Who did what, when, and why?* This may take a bit of practice!

**Comic Mix-Up** Build up your child's sequencing skills. Cut a comic strip into sections. Ask your child to put the strip in the correct order and to explain his or her thinking.

**Wonderful Window** Invite your child to look out of a window. Then ask: *What do you see that begins with the letter W?* See if your child can name five things. You can try this with other letters, as well.

**Travel Brochure** Together, you and your child can create a "travel brochure" for someplace you have been over the summer. For example, the place could be something as local as a neighborhood swimming pool or park, or a distant place that was part of a big vacation. Write about the place (or places) and remember to include pictures, either illustrated, images found in magazines, or if possible, real photographs.

**Your child might enjoy reading the following books.**

*Rent a Third Grader*
by B.B. Hiller

*The Scrambled States of America*
by Laurie Keller

*Ten True Animal Rescues*
by Jeanne Betancourt

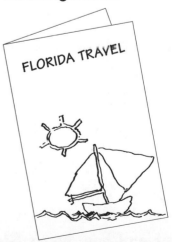

Special Note: The activity for Day 4 of this week is a mini-book. Have your child tear out the page along the perforation and cut along the dotted line. After he or she positions the two sections so the mini-book pages are in sequence, have him or her staple and fold to form a book. Then he or she can complete all the puzzles in the mini-book.

_____ **'s Incentive Chart: Week 10**
Name Here

This week, I plan to read _____ minutes each day.

CHART YOUR PROGRESS HERE.

| Week 10 | Day 1 | Day 2 | Day 3 | Day 4 | Day 5 |
|---------|-------|-------|-------|-------|-------|
| I read for... | minutes | minutes | minutes | minutes | minutes |
| Put a sticker to show you completed each day's work. | | | | | |

# Congratulations!

Wow! You did a great job this week!

#1

Place sticker here.

**Parent or Caregiver's Signature** _____

# Buckets of Fun

An **adjective** *helps you imagine how something looks, feels, smells, sounds, or tastes.*

Write a list of adjectives on each bucket to fit the bucket's category.

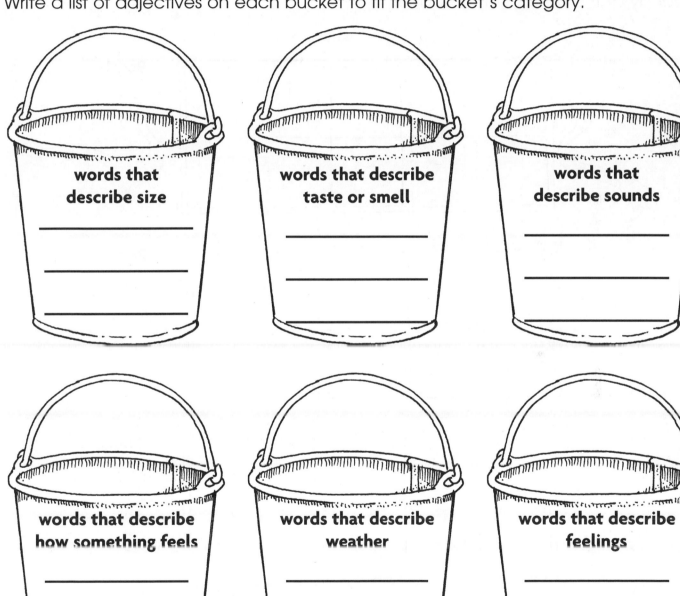

words that describe size

words that describe taste or smell

words that describe sounds

words that describe how something feels

words that describe weather

words that describe feelings

 Make a "mystery bag" by putting a secret object inside. Tell someone about the object inside using describing words!

Scholastic Teaching Resources    *Get Ready for 3rd Grade*

# Candy Boxes

Steve works in a candy store. He puts candy into boxes. Each box has 10 spaces. Steve has 32 candies. Try to draw 32 candies in the boxes below. Write the number of candies in each box on the line. Write the number of any leftover candy at the bottom of the page.

Box 1: _____

Box 2: _____

Box 3: _____

**Extra**

Leftover candies: _____

Scholastic Teaching Resources  *Get Ready for 3rd Grade*

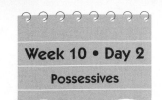

# Whose Is It?

A **noun** can show who owns something. To do this, add an **(')** and **-s**.

Joe is packing for a trip. He needs to pack everything on the list. Each object belongs to a different family member. Study the picture to learn who owns each thing. Then write it on the suitcase.

| skateboard | hat | bone |
| bowl | sunglasses | teddy bear |

1. _____    4. _____

2. _____    5. _____

3. _____    6. _____

Write a story about Joe's family and their trip on the back of this page.

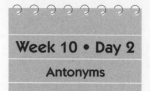

# The Opposite Of

Circle the correct word to complete each sentence.

1. Rich is the opposite of poor, and weak is the opposite of _____.

    A. strong          B. day          C. frail

2. Give is the opposite of take, and ask is the opposite of _____.

    A. get          B. answer          C. teacher

3. Help is the opposite of harm, and work is the opposite of _____.

    A. hurt          B. try          C. play

4. Good is the opposite of bad, and rough is the opposite of _____.

    A. smooth          B. bumpy          C. mean

5. Over is the opposite of under, and near is the opposite of _____.

    A. middle          B. far          C. here

6. Warm is the opposite of cool, and safe is the opposite of _____.

    A. afraid          B. cold          C. unsafe

7. Cloudy is the opposite of sunny, and early is the opposite of _____.

    A. late          B. day          C. timely

8. Top is the opposite of bottom, and front is the opposite of _____.

    A. whole          B. back          C. side

 **Discuss with someone why you did not choose the other words.**

Scholastic Teaching Resources   *Get Ready for 3rd Grade*

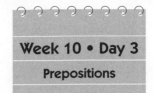

# Where Is It?

A **preposition** often helps tell where something is.

Study the picture. Find each item in the column on the left. Then draw a line to the words that tell where it is. The prepositions are underlined.

| **What** | **Where** |
|---|---|
| 1. chair | a. <u>above</u> the door |
| 2. bear | b. <u>on</u> the desk |
| 3. shoe | c. <u>under</u> the bed |
| 4. plane | d. <u>behind</u> the trash basket |
| 5. cat | e. <u>in</u> the bed |
| 6. computer | f. <u>at</u> the window |
| 7. dog | g. <u>near</u> the desk |
| 8. poster | h. <u>over</u> the bed |

Pick three objects from the picture and write a complete sentence to tell where each object is.

Scholastic Teaching Resources    Get Ready for 3rd Grade

# Wacky World

An asking sentence is called a **question**. It begins with a capital letter and ends with a question mark (?).

Write each question correctly.

1. **why is that car in a tree**

_____

2. **should that monkey be driving a bus**

_____

3. **did you see feathers on that crocodile**

_____

4. **can elephants really lay eggs**

_____

5. **is that my mother covered in spots**

_____

 **On another piece of paper, draw your own picture of a wacky world. Write two questions about your picture.**

Scholastic Teaching Resources   Get Ready for 3rd Grade

# Compound Roundup

Make as many compound words as you can by joining words in boxes that connect vertically, horizontally, or diagonally. Write your answers on a separate sheet of paper. **There are 20 compound words to round up in each puzzle.**

Name _____

**3**

| pen | play | hog | chair | high | window |
|---|---|---|---|---|---|
| stick | ground | wheel | arm | deep | way |
| yard | back | melon | lid | pit | drive |
| fall | water | brow | eye | ever | green |
| up | hot | ball | round | lash | house |

**6**

| fit | cycle | line | hall | flag | trip |
|---|---|---|---|---|---|
| motor | out | air | bell | way | pole |
| law | cap | side | knob | door | cone |
| burn | sun | walk | shoe | bone | pine |
| set | hot | shine | wish | fire | back |

**8**

| weed | shell | shore | stage | dragon | hole |
|---|---|---|---|---|---|
| food | sea | sick | fly | coach | scotch |
| top | cave | fire | proof | hop | butter |
| sand | car | man | place | fruit | vine |
| mail | box | shade | lamp | apple | grape |

## 2

| mill | wind | toe | tail | light | work |
|---|---|---|---|---|---|
| lady | bug | pig | pony | print | step |
| spread | bed | chop | class | mate | foot |
| tub | robe | room | stick | stool | mare |
| cold | bath | mush | way | time | night |

## 4

| pick | paste | ache | line | fore | over |
|---|---|---|---|---|---|
| drop | tooth | bird | head | how | moon |
| gum | cage | brush | some | light | saw |
| day | red | hair | thing | any | guard |
| home | dream | cut | body | life | where |

## 7

| skate | pull | quake | worm | pea | pit |
|---|---|---|---|---|---|
| board | over | blue | earth | suit | cock |
| surf | score | due | man | snow | case |
| bag | end | bench | see | storm | brief |
| week | bean | work | home | thing | brain |

## 5

| cuffs | shake | wear | every | stand | drop |
|---|---|---|---|---|---|
| fog | hand | ship | under | rain | card |
| kick | horn | pants | bow | board | fold |
| drum | ache | time | black | cup | bill |
| ear | stick | lip | cake | spoon | tea |

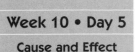

# Where the Sun Shines

Florida is known for its pleasant weather. In fact, it has earned the nickname "Sunshine State." As a result of its warm, sunny climate, Florida is a good place for growing fruits, such as oranges and grapefruits. Many older people go to live in Florida. They enjoy the good weather. Northerners on vacation also visit Florida for the same reason.

Read the paragraph. Then complete the cause-and-effect map.

**Effects**

**Cause**

**MORE!** During which season do most people probably go to Florida? Tell why you think so.

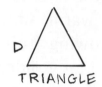

# Shape Gaper

FLAT SHAPES HAVE LENGTH AND WIDTH.

A SQUARE  B CIRCLE  C RECTANGLE  D TRIANGLE

SOLID SHAPES HAVE LENGTH AND WIDTH AND DEPTH.

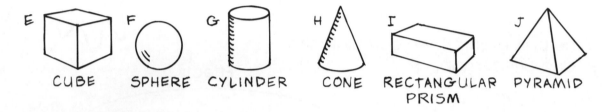

E CUBE  F SPHERE  G CYLINDER  H CONE  I RECTANGULAR PRISM  J PYRAMID

MATCH THE SHAPES WITH THESE OBJECTS. USE THE LETTERS ABOVE.

**A.**
1. BALL
2. WASTEBASKET
3. RING
4. POSTAGE STAMP
5. BIRDHOUSE
6. CRAYON BOX
7. ICE CUBE
8. APOLLO SPACECRAFT
9. TRASH BARREL
10. JAR
11. ENVELOPE

**B.**
1. COMPACT DISC
2. AN ORANGE
3. A PENNANT
4. A BUILDING
5. FISH BOWL
6. CHILD'S BLOCK
7. CHECKERS (GAME)
8. A SAIL ON A SMALL BOAT
9. CEREAL BOX
10. PLANET EARTH
11. STICK OF BUTTER

**C.**
1. ROAD MARKER
2. FLAG
3. SHEET OF PAPER
4. FLASHLIGHT
5. SOUP CAN
6. POSTER
7. BASEBALL
8. TRAIN CAR
9. A DIME
10. PHOTOGRAPH
11. WORLD GLOBE

Scholastic Teaching Resources  *Get Ready for 3rd Grade*

**Page 7**
1. baseball player: baseball, cap
2. football player: football, helmet
3. tennis player; tennis ball, racket
4. cyclist: bicycle, helmet
5. hockey player: hockey stick, ice skates

**Page 8**
1. tablecloth
2. popcorn
3. cookbook
4. applesauce
5. fruitcake
6. meatball
7. watermelon
8. blueberry
Answers will vary.

**Page 9**
2 + 8 = 10; 24 + 7 = 31; 32 + 9 = 41;
1 + 9 = 10; 7 + 4 = 11; 45 + 5 = 50;
31 + 4 = 35; 11 + 9 = 20; 17 + 9 = 26;
22 + 13 = 35; 26 + 6 = 32; 19 + 9 = 28;
11 + 7 = 18; 16 + 22 = 38; 31 + 11 = 42;
14 + 9 = 23; 12 + 7 = 19; 40 + 14 = 54;
27 + 6 = 33; 12 + 9 = 21; 4 + 8 = 12;
41 + 21 = 62; 37 + 31 = 68; 16 + 6 = 22;
16 + 5 = 21; 10 + 24 = 34; 20 + 21 = 41;
15 + 5 = 20

**Page 10**
1. The sun is the closest star to Earth.
2. The sun is not the brightest star.
3. What is the temperature of the sun?
4. The sun is a ball of hot gas.
5. How large is the sun?
6. Will the sun ever burn out?

**Page 11**
1. angry
2. west
3. parakeet
4. lemonade
5. arm
6. George
7. pudding
8. crayon
9. dime
Birds 3; Desserts 7; Bad Feelings 1; Boys'
Names 6; Money 9; School Supplies 8;
Directions 2; Body Parts 5; Drinks 4

**Page 12**
Dear Mom and Dad,
     Camp is so cool! Today we went
swimming. Do you know what the best part
of camp is? I think fishing is my favorite thing
to do. Did you feed my hamster? I really
miss you.
     Love, Dalton

Sentences will vary.

**Page 13**
68 – 26 = 42; 34 – 11 = 23; 19 – 12 = 7;
91 – 20 = 71; 47 – 15 = 32; 33 – 21 = 12;
69 – 59 = 10; 88 – 54 = 34; 67 – 13 = 54;
88 – 12 = 76; 97 – 13 = 84; 27 – 5 = 22;
28 – 24 = 4; 17 – 6 = 11; 35 – 11 = 24;
81 – 21 = 60; 57 – 55 = 2; 39 – 15 = 24;
60 – 10 = 50

**Page 14**
2, 1, 4, 3          Check child's work.

**Page 15**
3, 4, 1, 2          Check child's work.

**Page 16**
1. round
2. call
3. full
4. away
5. upon
6. pull

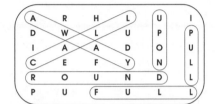

**Page 20**
1, 4, 6, 7, 10, 11, 14, 15, 18, 20, 21,
24, 26, teapot

**Page 22**
1. climb
2. shells
3. trail
4. hop
5. yelled
nose, goes, bows; long, song, wrong; trunk,
dunk, sunk; damp, camp, ramp; bumpy,
lumpy, humpy; trail, pail, sail, tail
Answers will vary.

**Page 23**
45 – 39 = 6; 84 – 59 = 25; 72 – 55 = 17;
71 – 19 = 52; 84 – 25 = 59; 60 – 18 = 42;
98 – 29 = 69; 74 – 15 = 59; 71 – 17 = 54;
88 – 29 = 59; 82 – 68 = 14; 91 – 32 = 59;
34 – 16 = 18; 92 – 13 = 79; 43 – 35 = 8;
57 – 28 = 29; She had 15 tickets left.

**Page 24**
1. camp
2. likes
3. walks
4. build
5. cook
6. crawl
Sentences will vary.

**Page 25**
Check child's work.

**Page 26**
1. B chair
2. A shirt
3. B clock
4. A peach
5. C face
6. A den
7. B sweater
8. C bike

**Page 27**
207 + 544 = 751; 126 + 89 = 215;
328 + 348 = 676; 257 + 458 = 715;
547 + 129 = 676; 624 + 127 = 751;
108 + 107 = 215; 229 + 418 = 647;
258 + 268 = 526; 379 + 336 = 715;
417 + 109 = 526; 153 + 494 = 647

**Page 28**
Sentences will vary.

**Page 32**
1. zoo, big
2. giraffe, tall
3. girls, two
4. spots, brown
color word: brown
size words: tall, big
number word: two

**Page 33**
1. A tell about Hsing-Hsing and Ling-Ling
2. and 3. Answers will vary.

**Page 34**
1. 4 + 5 = 9; 2. 11 – 6 = 5; 3. 9 + 7 = 16;
4. 4 + 8 = 12; 5. 3 – 2 = 1; 6. 7 + 7 = 14;
7. 15 – 10 = 5; 8. 2 + 8 = 10; 9. 5 – 2 = 3

**Page 35**
1. "Let's go on a picnic."
2. "That's a great idea."
3. "What should we bring?"
4. "We should bring food."
5. "Yes, let's bring lots and lots of food."
6. "You're no help at all!"
7. Sentences will vary.

**Page 36**
1. B hat
2. C grin
3. B tune
4. A pan
5. C damp
6. A glad
7. B quick
8. A nap

**Page 37**
A. $1.49 + $.50 + $.75 + $1.22 = $3.96
B. $1.72 + $.65 + $1.17 = $3.54
C. $1.86 + $1.84 + $.84 + $1.07 = $5.61
D. $1.53 + $1.90 + $1.22 + $.84 = $5.49
E. $1.86 + $.50 + $1.17 = $3.53
F. $1.49 + $.86 + $.75 = $3.10

**Page 38**
Answers will vary.

**Page 39**
Action words: found, call, find, put, pull
Direction words: away, below, upon,
around, behind, above
Answers will vary.

**Page 40**
1. willow
2. salute
3. pinwheel or comet

**Page 43**
Topic: Favorite Sandwiches for School
Lunches; Details: peanut butter and jelly,
ham, bologna, cheese, turkey

**Page 44**
1. thought
2. walk
3. bought
4. bring
5. draw
6. hold
7. talk
8. drew

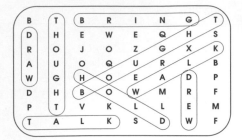

## Page 45

| | |
|---|---|
| 1. plays | 6. dives |
| 2. play | 7. climb |
| 3. runs | 8. climbs |
| 4. run | 9. throw |
| 5. dive | 10. throws |

## Page 46

Sentences will vary.

## Page 47

| | |
|---|---|
| 1. ounces | 9. pounds |
| 2. pounds | 10. ounces |
| 3. ounces | 11. ounces |
| 4. pounds | 12. pounds |
| 5. pounds | 13. pounds |
| 6. pounds | 14. ounces |
| 7. ounces | 15. ounces |
| 8. ounces | |

## Page 48

1. b. A pony costs a lot more than three dollars.
2. a. also
3. c. lost
4. c. type
5. a. between the words lonely and quiet.

## Page 49

1. B He is not wearing a helmet.
2. F Cares a lot about safety.
3. Answers will vary.

## Page 50

| Across | Down |
|---|---|
| 1. climbed | 1. called |
| 3. barked | 2. mixed |
| 5. helped | 4. kicked |
| 7. yelled | 6. played |
| 8. walked | |

Answers will vary.

## Page 51

1. 2, 4, 6, 8
2. 4, 8, 12, 16
3. 6, 12, 18, 24
4. 8, 16, 24, 32
5. 10, 20, 30, 40, 50, 60, 70, 80, 90, 100

## Page 52

Lists of words will vary.

## Page 55

Japan: white background, circle for sun; Both: red and white; Canada: white background with 2 red stripes, red maple leaf

## Page 56

| | |
|---|---|
| 1. is, now | 4. is, now |
| 2. are, now | 5. am, now |
| 3. were, past | 6. was, past |

## Page 58

1. 3; 2. 3; 3. 2

## Page 59

| | |
|---|---|
| 1. couldn't | 4. don't |
| 2. wasn't | 5. didn't |
| 3. aren't | Sentences will vary. |

## Page 60

1. board, bored
2. bear, bare
3. chili, chilly
4. guessed, guest
5. patience, patients
6. I'll meet you at eight in the morning.
7. Would you fix me some tea and a bowl of cereal?
8. My aunt and uncle lived overseas for two years in Madrid.
9. Alex was sick with the flu and missed a whole week of school.
10. I want to buy a new pair of shoes, but I do not have a cent left.

## Page 61

Upper Peninsula: big forests, minerals; Both: attract tourists, part of Michigan, surrounded by Great Lakes;
Lower Peninsula: more people and large cities, most of industry

## Page 62

We have ~~grate~~ great stuff and big bargains!

Office ~~Supplys~~ Supplies
• Big boxes of old newspaper
• Ballpoint pens that are out of ink
• Broken rubber bands
• Empty printer ink containers

Household Goods
• Old phon**e** books
• Torn sheets
• Old toothbrushes
• Empty ~~pante~~ paint cans
• Chipped plates
• A bunch of old pizza box**e**s

Clothing
• Single left shoes
• Socks with ho**l**es
• Jackets with broken zippers
• Sleeves that were cut off a shirt

F**u**rniture and Hardware
• A box of bent nails
• A saggy bed
• A sofa with mice living in it
• A ~~chare~~ chair with only three legs
• A TV with only one channel
• Old do**o**r knobs

## Page 63

1. 9; 2. 22; 3. 17; 4. 45; 5. 67; 6. 108; 7. 86; 8. 153; 9. 370; 10. 534
Where do cows go for entertainment? To the "moo"vies

## Page 64

1. The party was fun and exciting.
2. We blew up orange and red balloons.
3. We ate cake and ice cream.
4. The cake frosting was green and yellow.
5. We made a bookmark and a clay pot.
6. We brought games and prizes.

## Page 68

| | |
|---|---|
| 1. teeth | 4. sharp |
| 2. mouth | 5. grin |
| 3. close | |

clean, bean, mean, seen; jaws, claws, laws; start, dart, cart; grin, win, fin, pin; wide, hide, ride; stood, good, hood

## Page 69

Check child's work.

## Page 70

| | |
|---|---|
| 1. has | 6. had |
| 2. have | 7. had |
| 3. had | 8. have |
| 4. have | 9. has |
| 5. has | |

## Page 71

Child's answers will vary.

## Page 72

Child's answers will vary.

## Page 73

Hitting a Ball: golf, tennis, lacrosse; Throwing a Ball: basketball, bowling; Kicking a Ball: soccer, football, rugby, kickball

## Page 74

| | |
|---|---|
| 1. She | 4. He |
| 2. They | 5. It |
| 3. We | |

## Page 75

1. 7:35, 35 minutes after 7, 25 minutes to 8
2. 3:50, 50 minutes after 3, 10 minutes to 4
3. 9:15, 15 minutes after 9, 45 minutes to 10
4. 6:25, 25 minutes after 6, 35 minutes to 7
5. 9:55, 55 minutes after 9, 5 minutes to 10
6. 2:05, 5 minutes after 2, 55 minutes to 3

## Page 76

Child's answers will vary.

## Page 79

A. 2/2 matches the triangle, 2/12 matches the rectangle, 2/3 matches the circle
B. color 1/2 circle, color the whole rectangle

## Page 80
A. 1. Q; 2. S; 3. S; 4. Q; 5. Q; 6. S; 7. S; 8. Q
B. 1. How did the ant carry the crumb?
2. She carried it herself.

## Page 81
BL: blue, black, blink, blob, blanket, blimp;
GR: green, gray, grumpy; TR: try, tray, trick,
truck; SM: smoke, smile, smell, smack

## Page 82
1. Fill a cup with water and add some
flower seeds. 2. This will soften the seeds
because they are hard. 3. Fill a cup with dirt
while the seeds soak in water. 4. Bury the
seeds in the cup until the dirt covers them.
5. Add water to the plant but do not add
too much. 6. Set the cup in the sun so the
plant will grow.

## Page 83

## Page 84
1. new, newer, newest
2. small, smaller, smallest
3. warm, warmer, warmest
4. round, rounder, roundest
5. neat, neater, neatest
6. soft, softer, softest

## Page 85
Cause: birds eating seeds;
First Effect: put brown belts in garden; Other
Effects: birds thought belts were snakes,
birds stayed away from garden, plants grew
in peace

## Page 86
1. took
2. was
3. saw
4. many
5. brought
6. seen
7. has
8. are
9. were
10. saw
11. wore
12. going
13. Does
14. brought

## Page 87
A. 2 x 3 = 6; B. 3 x 3 = 9; C. 4 x 2 = 8;
D. 3 x 5 = 15; E. 1 x 3 = 3; F. 4 x 3 = 12;
G. 2 x 6 = 12; H. 3 x 4 = 12; I. 3 x 6 = 18;
J. 5 x 3 = 15; K. 5 x 1 = 5; L. 7 x 2 = 14;
Check array. 24 people

## Page 88

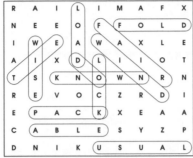

| R | A | I | L | I | M | A | F | X |
| N | E | E | O | F | F | O | L | D |
| I | W | E | A | W | A | X | L | E |
| A | I | X | D | L | I | I | O | T |
| T | S | K | N | O | W | N | R | N |
| R | E | V | O | C | Z | R | D | I |
| E | P | A | C | K | X | E | A | A |
| C | A | B | L | E | S | Y | Z | P |
| D | N | I | K | U | S | U | A | L |

1. unusual        4. unfold
2. untie          5. unwise
3. unlock         6. unfair

## Page 91
Writing a poem
Is like riding a bike
Once you start riding
You ride where you like.

For exampe, I can write
Any wurd I want here
As long as it rhymes
And soundes good to the ear.

I can write in any style
I can write in any spede
As long as my readrs
Continue to read.

There's
There is only one danger
One risk that I run
When I sense that my readers
Have stoped having fun.
At this point its best
Not to delay
Simply kick up your kickstand
And just ride eway.

## Page 92
A. 1. S; 2. S; 3. P; 4. S; 5. P
B. 1. baby, sisters 2. nightgown, pockets
3. hand, fingers 4. baby, parents
5. family, girls
C. Singular: train, cow; Plural: fences, gates

## Page 93
Main Idea: The Milky Way is our galaxy.
Details: 1. stars 2. outer 3. spiral 4. white
5. planets 6. 200

## Page 94
Across                Down
1. word               2. own
3. clean              3. carry
4. warm               6. again
5. ready

## Page 95
A. 2/10   B. 6/10   C. 7/10

## Page 96
A. 1. E; 2. C; 3. C; 4. E; 5. E.; 6. C;
7. E; 8. C
B. Answers will vary.

## Page 97
1. A on vacation
2. To get help for JoAnne
3. J friend
4. Answers will vary.

## Page 98
Answers will vary.

## Page 99
A. 2 x 4 = 8          I. 2 x 6 = 12
B. 3 x 3 = 9          J. 8 x 3 = 24
C. 3 x 5 = 15         K. 3 x 6 = 18
D. 4 x 3 = 12         L. 4 x 5 = 20
E. 4 x 1 = 4          M. 2 x 2 = 4
F. 6 x 3 = 18         N. 6 x 1 = 6
G. 8 x 2 = 16         O. 5 x 4 = 20
H. 6 x 4 = 24         P. 7 x 2 = 14
Check diagram. 35 hamburgers

## Page 100
Sentences will vary.

## Page 103
Dear Friend,
    My job as the first president of the
United States was hard. My friends and I
had to make new laws, new money, and
new jobs. The capital was in New York when
I became president. The it moved to
Philadelphia. Is the capital still there? Who is
the president today? I would love to see
how the United States has changed over
the past two hundred years!
    Sincerely,
    George Washington

## Page 104
A. 3 x 5 = 15         I. 5 x 3 = 15
B. 4 x 6 = 24         J. 4 x 10 = 40
C. 2 x 8 = 16         K. 5 x 1 = 5
D. 4 x 2 = 8          L. 3 x 11 = 33
E. 3 x 7 = 21         M. 4 x 8 = 32
F. 4 x 4 = 16         N. 4 x 0 = 0
G. 3 x 9 = 27         O. 4 x 12 = 48
H. 5 x 5 = 25         P. 4 x 9 = 36
24 items

## Page 105
A. 1. common
   2. common
   3. proper
B. 1. brother, sister; April
   2. names; Julius, May
   3. parents; Taiwan
   4. school; April, Saturday
   5. language; Mandarin
   6. book; May, Middle Ages
C. Common Nouns: camp, children, picnic
   Proper Nouns: August, David,
   Fourth of July

## Page 106
1. S  2. F  3. S  4. S  5. F  6. F  7. S
8. F  9. F  10. F  11. S  12. S

## Page 107
A. 2, 1, 3          F. 3, 1, 2
B. 1, 3, 2          G. 1, 3, 2
C. 3, 2, 1          H. 2, 1, 3
D. 2, 1, 3          I. 2, 1, 4
E. 3, 1, 2          J. 2, 4, 1, 3

## Page 108
A. 1. sparkling     4. Busy
   2. clear          5. fresh
   3. Large
B. Answers may include:
   1. red            4. loud
   2. soccer         5. sour
   3. sweet

## Page 109
1. venomous        5. rattlesnakes
2. sneaky          6. sand
3. camouflage      7. coral snake;
4. jungle             Watch out for sneaky
                      snakes!

## Page 110
1. C green         5. B square
2. A glass         6. A small
3. A winding       7. B clear
4. C red           8. C soft

## Page 111
1. effect          11. error
2. fun             12. pots
3. cup             13. chips
4. sugar           14. shine
5. lost            15. business
6. name            16. right
7. gentlemen       17. alive
8. order           18. cents
9. sweet           19. bacon
10. easy           20. sooner

## Page 112
A. 5 pennies equal 5 cents, one nickel
equals 5 cents
B. 10 pennies equal 10 cents, 2 nickels equal
10 cents, one dime equals 10 cents
C. 25 pennies equal 25 cents, 5 nickels
equal 25 cents, one quarter equals 25 cents

## Page 115
Lists of words will vary.

## Page 116
10, 10, 10, 2

## Page 117
1. Kevin's skateboard    4. Dad's sunglasses
2. Sam's bowl            5. Fred's bone
3. Emma's teddy bear     6. Mom's hat

## Page 118
1. A strong        5. B far
2. B answer        6. C unsafe
3. C play          7. A late
4. A smooth        8. B back

## Page 119
1. g. near the desk
2. e. in the bed
3. d. behind the trash basket
4. h. over the bed
5. f. at the window
6. b. on the desk
7. c. under the bed
8. a. above the door

## Page 120
1. Why is that car in a tree?
2. Should that monkey be driving a bus?
3. Did you see feathers on that crocodile?
4. Can elephants really lay eggs?
5. Is that my mother covered in spots?

## Page 121 and 122
p. 2: windmill, taillight, ladybug, pigtail,
ponytail, bedbug, bedspread, bedroom,
chopstick, classmate, classroom, footprint,
footstep, footstool, bathtub, bathrobe,
bathroom, mushroom, nightmare, nighttime

p. 3: playpen, playground, highchair,
highway, groundhog, wheelchair, armchair,
armpit, yardstick, background, backyard,
driveway, watermelon, waterfall, eyelid,
eyebrow, eyeball, eyelash, evergreen,
greenhouse

p. 4: forehead, toothpick, toothpaste,
toothache, toothbrush, birdcage,
headache, headline, headlight, moonlight,
gumdrop, somehow, something, daydream,
hairbrush, haircut, anything, anybody,
anywhere, lifeguard

p. 5: foghorn, handcuffs, handshake,
underwear, understand, underpants,
raindrop, rainbow, cardboard, drumstick,
blackboard, cupboard, cupcake, billboard,
billfold, eardrum, earache, lipstick, teacup,
teaspoon

p. 6: hallway, flagpole, motorcycle, outfit,
outline, outlaw, outside, airline, sidewalk,
doorbell, doorway, doorknob, sunburn,
sunset, sunshine, shoeshine, pinecone,
wishbone, backbone, backfire

p. 7: skateboard, pullover, peacock,
overboard, overdue, earthquake,
earthworm, suitcase, cockpit, surfboard,
scoreboard, snowsuit, snowman, snowstorm,
briefcase, weekend, beanbag, workbench,
homework, brainstorm

p. 8: stagecoach, dragonfly, seaweed,
seashell, seashore, seafood, seasick,
caveman, firefly, fireproof, fireman,
fireplace, hopscotch, butterscotch,
sandbox, mailbox, boxcar, lampshade,
grapefruit, grapevine

## Page 123
Cause: Florida has warm, sunny climate;
Effects: called "Sunshine State;"
good for growing oranges and grapefruit;
older people go to live there; vacationers
visit there

## Page 124
A. 1F, 2G, 3B, 4C or A, 5E, 6I, 7E, 8H, 9G,
10G, 11C
B. 1B, 2F, 3D, 4E, 5F, 6E, 7A, 8D, 9I, 10F, 11I
C. 1H, 2C, 3C, 4G, 5G, 6C, 7F, 8I, 9B, 10C or
A, 11F

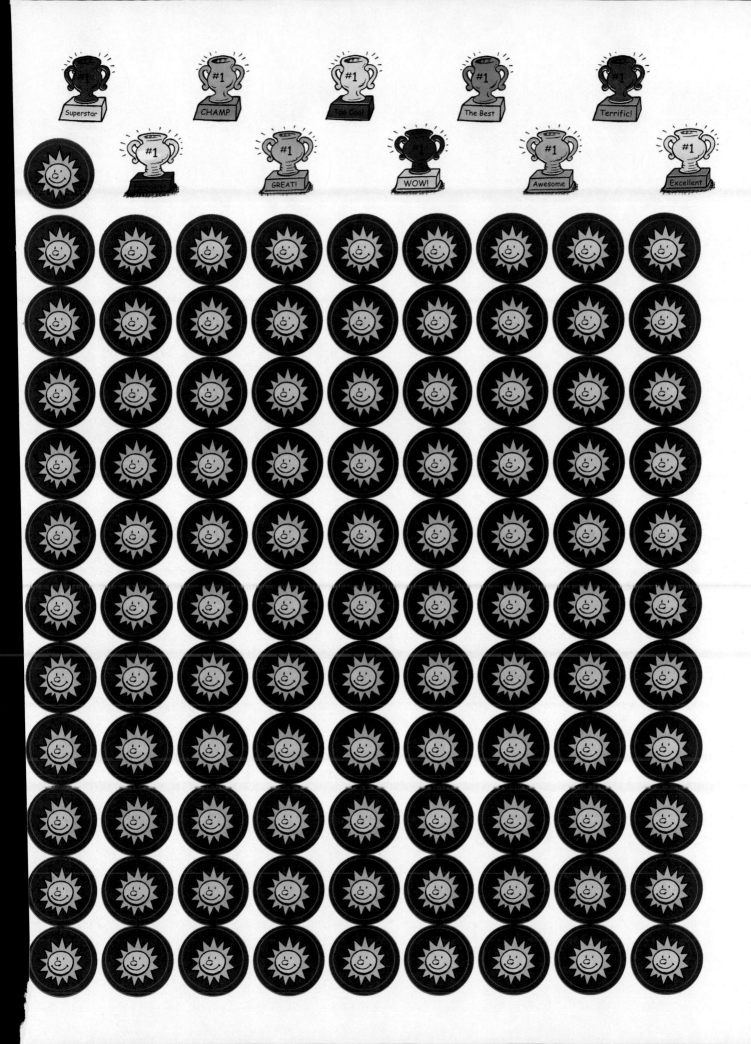